MYRON ARMS

Cathedral of the World

Myron Arms is a teacher, writer, and professional sailor who contributes regularly to *Cruising World*, *Sail*, and many other sailing and adventure magazines. Educated at both Yale and the Harvard Divinity School, he taught high school English for seven years before founding a sailing program for teenagers. As a U.S. Coast Guard–licensed ocean master since 1977, he has voyaged more than 100,000 sea miles and has led seven sail-training expeditions to northern Canada, Greenland, and the Arctic. He is the author of *Riddle of the Ice*.

ALSO BY MYRON ARMS

Riddle of the Ice

Cathedral of the World

MYRON ARMS

Cathedral of the World

Sailing Notes for a Blue Planet

ANCHOR BOOKS

A DIVISION OF RANDOM HOUSE, INC.   NEW YORK

FIRST ANCHOR BOOKS EDITION, APRIL 2000

Anchor Books and colophon are registered trademarks of
Random House, Inc.

The lines from "Humanity i love you" copyright 1925, 1953, © 1991 by the
Trustees for the E. E. Cummings Trust. Copyright © 1976 by George James
Firmage, from *Complete Poems: 1904–1962* by E. E. Cummings, Edited by George
J. Firmage. Reprinted by permission of Liveright Publishing Corporation.

The Library of Congress has cataloged the Doubleday edition as follows:
Arms, Myron.
Cathedral of the world: sailing notes for a blue planet
By Myron Arms. — 1st ed.
p. cm.
Includes bibliographical references
1. Seafaring life.   2. Voyages and travels.   3. Sailors—Religious life.
1. Title.
G540.A815   1999
910.4′5—dc21   98-27557
CIP

ISBN-13: 978-0-385-49476-2

Author photograph © Kay Arms

www.anchorbooks.com

Printed in the United States of America

146866421

For my three children Steve, Dave, and Chris;
and for theirs

Acknowledgments

Several essays in this collection first appeared in the following periodicals: "Charts and Other Fiction" in a shorter version in *Sail* (July 1993); "The Tunnel" in *Cruising World* (May 1990); certain sections of "Day Twenty-Two" under the title "Climbing the North Atlantic Hills" in *Sail* (February 1986). The essay "Ukivik Island" first appeared in slightly different form as a chapter in *Riddle of the Ice: A Scientific Adventure into the Arctic* (Anchor Doubleday, 1998).

I wish to thank the editors of all these publications for their encouragement and support, especially Bernadette Bernon at *Cruising World* and Rob McQuilkin, my wonderful editor and literary alter ego at Anchor Doubleday.

Contents

Contents

Preface

For centuries sailors who have voyaged to distant coasts have returned from their travels with written accounts of their experiences. Some of these have been technical notes. Some have been navigational logs. Some have been anecdotal descriptions of day to day events and encounters. Some have been all of these and more: philosophical musings whose purpose has been to explore the primal spaces and to articulate, for the rest of us, the sailor's age-old quest to understand his world and himself.

I have been fortunate to have traveled many thousands of miles in a small sailboat and to have found the time to reflect and write about these travels. The sailing started when I was a child. It was a gift given to me by my father on windy summer afternoons in an old wooden sloop called *Curlew*. It continued as a sequence of jobs working around sailboats, then as a series of long summer voyages with my wife Kay and our three children.

Later, during the late 1970s and early 1980s, I served

as skipper of a sail-training school for teenage boys and girls aboard a traditional wood schooner called *Dawn Treader*. Afterward came an opportunity to build my own boat and to sail her more than sixty thousand sea miles around the top of the northern Atlantic, visiting some of the wildest and least accessible coasts in the world and returning with a rare and valuable commodity: an experience of wilderness.

Sometime during these travels—I'm not quite sure when—I began putting together a notebook of essays, letters, and other short pieces about some of the places I'd sailed and some of the ideas and speculations that had happened along the way. At the time I wasn't particularly worried about how all the parts of the notebook were going to fit together. Some were essays I had written for my children. Some were letters to friends and other people I had sailed with. Some were fragments from longer works. Some were articles already published elsewhere.

Over the years I've come to realize that the pieces I've been collecting are actually a set of sailing notes of the sort that mariners have kept for generations. Many of these notes are reflective and metaphorical. Some of the voyages they chronicle are interior. But all share a common destination, a place I've come to think of as "the cathedral of the world." This is a setting that is everywhere and that anyone can visit: a geographical location, a frame of mind, a promise.

Taken individually, the sailing notes that follow recount many separate voyages. Taken together, they describe a single voyage—the same one that millions of us make as we seek to learn how this planet works and what our place in it should be.

We, all of us, are living in a dangerous time—perhaps the most dangerous time that our species has ever known. Many of the problems we face, I'm convinced, lie rooted deep in our past and have to do with stories we have told ourselves for thousands of years about who we are and how we are related to the Earth. Solutions are possible. But they will happen, I believe, only as we learn to reinterpret the old stories, challenge the old paradigms, and search for new ones.

The notes and speculations that follow are dedicated to this challenge and this search—and to the generations that will accomplish them.

—MYRON ARMS
May 1998

Cathedral of the World

Clouds are not spheres . . . Mountains are not cones. Lightning does not travel in a straight line. The new geometry mirrors a universe that is rough, not rounded, scabrous, not smooth. It is a geometry of the pitted, pocked, and broken up, the twisted, tangled, and intertwined.

—JAMES GLEICK, *Chaos*

Forest Light

On a citadel overlooking the Spanish city of Grenada, there stands a magnificent Moorish palace called the Alhambra. A few years ago during a sailing voyage to southern Spain I was able to spend a day visiting this place, strolling through its ornate chambers, gazing at its fountain courts. The Alhambra is an artistic *tour de force* that the guidebooks describe as one of the great architectural wonders of the world.

Visitors here are awed by the intricate geometry of

the place, the counterpoint of line and form, the symmetry of every wall and arch and promenade that makes this building what it is: a monument to arithmetic predictability. I was also awed—but not in the way the guidebooks suggested. The longer I lingered, the more uneasy I felt. I found myself wondering what it would be like to actually *live* in a setting like this, surrounded by room after room of neurotic filigree. I began to feel as if I were a prisoner in some sort of compulsive Arabian nightmare. The walls, the floors, the perfectly proportioned windows and doors seemed to close in around me, and I felt I was about to suffocate . . .

For me—and I'm certain for many others—the Alhambra is too predictable, too symmetrical, too carefully organized. The day I visited there I found myself longing for a glimpse of white towering clouds, a craggy mountaintop, a twisted and gnarled old tree—anything random and disorderly. I didn't feel right again until I had left the ornate confines of that building and walked through a stand of elms on the hillside below. The November sunlight slanted through the leaves and flickered in odd patterns at my feet. For the first time in many hours, I felt I could relax again.

What was it that was so unsettling to me that day on the hilltop in Grenada? What was it about that Moorish conceptualization of paradise-on-Earth that felt so confining? And what was it about the sunlight dancing on the forest floor that seemed to provide the spiritual antidote? The answers to these questions, I suspect, may point the way toward some important things that I am seeking in this world and may help to explain the way I want to live.

Think for a minute about the experience of randomness: the dance of flames in an open fireplace, the endless progression of clouds moving across a summer sky, the sound of surf breaking along a beach, the crisscrossing of seas on the surface of the ocean, the flight of birds on a windy autumn afternoon. Like the patterns of sunlight flickering on the forest floor, each of these experiences is chaotic and open-ended. Their attraction lies in their unpredictability. They are as unlike the closed and predictable geometries of the Alhambra as it is possible to be.

And they surround us everywhere. They are the splay of veins in a leaf, the tracing of a heartbeat on an oscilloscope, the silhouette of branches against a gray winter sky, the turbulence of the wind during a tempest at sea, the lines of grain in a beautifully polished piece of wood.

They are, in short, what the natural world seems to be about in thousands of its moods and faces.

One of the questions that I find myself asking about all such experiences is the obvious one: if they are so chaotic and unpredictable, why aren't they also terrifying? Why do so many people gaze into the fire, stare at the clouds, listen to the wind, watch the flight of birds?

Why do these experiences often seem restful and comforting? Why don't we flee from them? Why aren't we confounded by their apparent complexity?

Some are. Some want to live in Alhambras of the mind—with everything orderly and predictable. Some seek for the truth primarily in closed systems, in questions with simple answers, in perfect geometric shapes. These are the ones Henry James must have been referring to when he observed that "the rule of nature is chaos—the dream of man is order."

But there are others—many others—who find in their dreams the siren song of chaos. These are the fire gazers, the ocean voyagers, the forest walkers.

I want to live among the forest walkers. I want to celebrate the chaos of nature, the randomness, the endless permutations of an inscrutable universe. I want to experience the tempest and feel the edges of my ability to comprehend.

Why? Not because I think the tempest is really incomprehensible. But because I have an enduring suspicion that the tempest is utterly simple and—on some deep, subverbal level—thoroughly comprehensible. Call it an intuition. Call it a strange and compelling trust in what is.

The fingers of the fire, the rage of the tempest, the mottled dance of forest light: each is an expression of an orderliness far beyond the ability of our rational minds to comprehend. We do not understand their endless permutations—yet the intuition remains. They are simple. They are "orderly" on some barely accessible level. We can't explain them—but many can feel their truth.

As a sailor, one of the things I often wonder about while standing behind the helm of a little boat in a deep, rolling sea is the feeling of knowing what motion will happen next. There is nothing orderly or predictable about the rise and fall of crossing waves, the surging of the hull, the continual changes in wind velocity and direction. Yet for many who have sailed on the ocean there is a familiarity about the patterns that evolve—as familiar as the subtle variations of one's own heartbeat—that results in a kind of perpetual déjà vu. This feeling is enhanced when sailing at night, for then the patterns are translated directly through the senses of balance and hearing and touch upward into the brain. Whether one is sailing in the clear midnight of a million stars or in the deafening roar of a gale, the feeling persists. The feeling of *knowing* this motion, of understanding the principles of its organization.

Such an experience is not without its own kind of terror—because the patterns are so impersonal. Because at any time there might come (and some day there will come) the conflagration, the bolt of lightning, the rogue sea that will neither know nor care about one's own ego, one's precious little-self. And then the irregular pulse in the stream of time that each conceives as his own individual being will be swirled back into the cauldron of experience, consumed by the fire, overwhelmed by the forest, drowned in the storm.

These things are and will be. They are not rational. They are not predictable or orderly. But they are true—and because they are true, they are worthy of our attention, our contemplation, our wonder.

I do not want to live in a convenient geometry. I do not want to force experience into a systematized catechism of simple questions and simple answers. I do not want to travel across time according to an incomplete map that fails to confront the frontiers.

I want to live among the fire gazers and the ocean voyagers and the forest walkers and learn the secret that they know (or suspect) about the order beyond the chaos. I want to celebrate a deity that encompasses all there is—not one that insulates us from the terror—and magnificence—of unpredictability. I want to believe beyond the rationality of our times, to trust the night-feeling of the spirit, to sense—with the fire and the waves and the dance of forest light—the exquisite geometry of an inscrutable universe infinitely chaotic, infinitely simple.

"What is the hardest thing of all?" asked Goethe—and answered: "What seems the easiest to you: to use your eyes and see what is in front of them."
—THEODORE ROSZAK, *Where the Wasteland Ends*

Charts and Other Fiction

Some of my earliest memories are of games I used to play with my father on long winter evenings, the two of us hunched over a table in our living room studying the charts for the next sailing trip he was always planning for the family during his upcoming holiday. Armed with a pencil and a set of parallel rules, we would set sail on imaginary voyages across the bays of summer, marking off distances and estimated times of arrival, checking depths and the location of buoys, poking into coves, making plans.

The thing I remember most about my father's charts was the way they set us free. They were like novels without characters: settings in which we were the actors and the creators of our own episodes. They contained fabulous worlds, and we lived in them like supermen, traveling through their benign geography as if we were invincible.

There seemed no reason, then, to worry about the dangers that might have been lurking somewhere within the games we played. The games themselves seemed harmless enough. In fact, they seemed a perfect way for a little boy and his father to share a few pleasant hours together. I wasn't concerned at the time about the inconsistencies between the charts and the actual geography they were intended to represent. I wasn't thinking about the *real* bays of summer: the ones with uncharted ledges and misplaced buoys and currents that flowed in opposite directions to the ones predicted by the cartographers.

As a child I learned to roam across the worlds of my father's charts careless and free. But I didn't learn about their limitations. I didn't realize that nautical charts, like all maps, are only guidebooks: fictitious renderings of a world perceived by imperfect human beings, never identical with the actual places they describe. I learned about the wealth of information the charts contained. But I didn't learn that they were also filled with oversights and half-truths and miscalculations. This realization has taken many years to learn—years of trial and error, summers of close calls, winters of near catastrophe when I've made the mistake of trusting the chart spread out before me, only to discover that the cartographer must have been half asleep the day he drew this line or marked that shoal or measured such and such a distance.

Nautical charts suffer from a basic flaw: the flaw of scale. They are complicated, often powerful abstractions of the actual world, but they are not—cannot be—identical with that world. The terrain they attempt to map is too large and too complex. To be useful at all, they must reduce and simplify.

The Polish-American mathematician Benoit Mandelbrot once asked an odd question whose implications may have forever changed the face of modern mathematics: "How long is the coast of Britain?" The answer, he argued, is not to be found on any chart. In fact, the answer is not to be found in any conclusive way at all, at least not with the tools of measurement that we have presently available to us.

The reason for this apparent dilemma has to do with scale. Imagine a cartographer armed with a measuring device one meter in length. He paces off the coastline in question one meter at a time, traveling in and out of bays, across rocky headlands, over river deltas, until he comes up with a total number of meters. Now imagine the same cartographer with a much shorter measuring device, say one centimeter in length. This time as he remeasures the distance, his total will include more detail. His new "coastline" will include pebbles and rocks that were ignored in his first calculation, and the resulting answer will be somewhat greater.

What Mandelbrot discovered was that there seemed to be no limit to the length of the coastline, providing only that the scale of measurement could be made smaller each time. A microscopic measuring stick would reveal as yet undetected bays and promontories that would, when measured on a smaller scale, contain ever smaller bays and promontories, all the way down to sub-atomic scales (and possibly beyond). The point he was trying to convey, as a mathematician, had to do with the tendency of certain apparently chaotic natural phenomena (such as "coastlines") to repeat complex patterns across scale. But what he also managed to show was the impossibility of anyone's ever drawing a perfectly accurate chart of any real coastline anywhere on Earth.

Chart makers, all of them, are the purveyors of our collective nostalgia for order and simplicity. They are players in a con-game whose performance is so convincing that we are, at least momentarily, blinded to the underlying dishonesty of their craft. Each line a chart maker draws is an approximation. Each location is a calculated guess. Each measurement is a hypothetical proposition whose accuracy is based partially on the calibration of the measuring device, partially on the attentiveness of the one who reads the scale.

Even when we know such things, however, we seem willing to suspend our disbelief. We *want* things simple. We want to think that we can comprehend the world that the chart represents. So we accept the chart maker's fiction—we welcome his lie.

I remember the first time I was forced to question the chart maker's world. I was eleven years old. For two summers I'd been learning how to sail with my father and uncles and older cousins in a small wooden dinghy in the river in front of my grandmother's house. Finally, I was given permission to sail the boat on my own. I wasn't allowed to venture out around Stone Point into Buzzards Bay—the seas were too rough out there, my father warned, and the afternoon winds were too strong. But I could sail in the river and investigate its creeks and coves to my heart's content. I was given the key to the boathouse where the dinghy was kept and a chart of the river, and I was set free to unravel the mysteries of a miniature world that seemed to me as large as all the seven seas.

The river, at first, felt strange and dangerous. Directly in front of my grandmother's house, between her beach and the cottages on Cromeset Point, was an irregular heap of broken granite rubble called the Channel Rocks. A quarter mile upriver was Indian Cove, marked on its southern flank by a sentinel boulder and surrounded by a series of shallow underwater ledges. In the first bend of the river was a low, muddy island of eelgrass flats that I had visited several times in a skiff to collect fiddler crabs for fishing. Beyond the island lay a series of shallow bays fringed with scrub pine and marsh grass, and beyond these were the twin highway bridges, a broken pier, and a half dozen gray shingle buildings: the last signs of human habitation before the river narrowed and twisted into a dark, unruly forest of pine and beech and pin oak.

My first attempts at navigating the river were tentative in the extreme. I studied my chart and kept as well as I could to mid-channel. All the obvious dangers—the Channel Rocks, the boulders and ledges at Indian Cove, the eelgrass shallows near the muddy island—were marked on the chart, and I gave each one a wide berth. I sailed on mornings when the weather was clear and the winds were light, increasing the range of my travels only as I grew familiar with major landmarks and with the look and feel of the river.

Familiarity is the enemy of care, however, and my boldness grew with the summer. The inevitable day of reckoning came in the last week of August when a cousin arrived at my grandmother's house for a visit. He had seldom sailed the river and knew even less than I did about its secrets, yet his presence gave me courage. He took the chart, I took the tiller, and we set off on the bottom of a flood tide one windy afternoon to explore all the way to the river's headwaters, promising our parents only that we would be home by dinnertime.

The upriver leg was easy. The wind was at our backs, and the current flooded strong in midstream. The boat seemed to fly on invisible wings as we ran past Indian Cove, around muddy island, under the highway bridge, past the last of the summer cottages, and into the cool shadows of the river's upper reaches.

But the homeward leg was a different story. Now the wind was ahead, and the only way to work the boat back downriver was to trim the sheet close-hauled and sail in a zigzag course across the channel. In the deep water the flooding tide now became our foe, and whatever progress we managed to make while we were in the relatively still water near the shore was quickly negated each time we were forced to cross the stream. It soon became apparent that if we hoped to get home by the time we'd promised, we were going to need to keep to the shallows and short-tack down the edges of the river.

The first rock we hit resounded against the wooden dagger board and sent a shudder through the hull that threw me forward against a thwart and skinned my knee.

My cousin laughed; I got angry. "Watch the chart," I yelled. "You're the navigator!"

The next rock glanced off the dagger board and caught under the heel of the rudder. The boat stopped dead in the water, and I hollered out my anger again.

"Okay, *you* read the chart," my cousin cried. "I can't figure it out."

We changed places, and I stared at the map as the boat gathered way, pointing my finger in a direction that I thought would lead us out of danger. A minute later we bounced off another rock, and another. My anger turned to frustration, then confusion, then fear. I stared at the chart. There were no rocks indicated in this cove, just a broken line where the marsh grass met the water and a single sounding somewhere in the middle. I began to suspect that nobody had ever really tried to map this part of the river. Either that—or else we were lost, and I was looking at the wrong section of the chart altogether.

"Try over there," I said, pointing across to the opposite shore. "I think we might've missed a turn." My cousin's laughter trickled to a groan as the boat shuddered and ricocheted off another boulder.

An hour later, after the dagger-board trunk had split apart and a seam had started to open along the keel, neither of us was laughing any longer. The dinghy was sinking. I had long since discarded the chart in favor of a bailing scoop. I tried to keep ahead of the leaks while my cousin sailed randomly among the shallows at the river's edge and the boat literally beat itself to pieces against a maze of hidden dangers.

Our progress was snail-like. The sun dropped below the tops of the trees, their long, purple shadows growing across the surface of the water, and I began to cry. Not so much out of fear, I think, as out of frustration and shame. I had placed my faith in a tool that had failed me. I had broken the trust I'd been given—and now I'd broken the boat as well.

When my father showed up just before dark in the fishing skiff to tow us back home, I could barely look him in the eye. But for some reason he didn't seem angry. He throttled back the outboard engine as he pulled alongside, and he peered down at the water rising in our bilges. "Looks like you boys have had a pretty rough afternoon," was all he said.

I started trying to explain—about the headwind, the contrary current, the chart that didn't work.

"Seems you've learned a lesson or two," he observed, nodding his head in sympathy. He tossed me a short length of towing line to tie around the cleat in the bow. "Sit in the stern and bail while I tow you slow. It's time to get home. Your mother has dinner waiting."

I've learned a few important things about nautical charts in the forty-odd years that have passed since that difficult afternoon in the river in front of my grandmother's house. I've learned that in order to use charts properly, you must be willing to move through the world they describe with a fair degree of uncertainty. You must treat the charts with respect—for often they contain the only available clues as to the shape of the territory ahead. But you must also learn to regard them with a lively skepticism: a kind of buffer zone of doubt that you wear about your being like an invisible suit of armor and that you use to test the actual data of your experience.

Credulity and skepticism: strange bedfellows. Taken together, they often result in an even stranger cast of mind, an irreverent perspective on the world in which the things you presume to know—all of them—take on a kind of compelling beauty and internal logic even as they also smack of the irrational and the absurd.

Nautical charts were my introduction to just such an irreverent cast of mind—one that I've lived with, for better or for worse, ever since. They were the first maps I ever came to love, and the first I learned to mistrust. To this day they contain an irresistible magnetism for me. They describe a world full of mystery and truth, a credible world that I find myself voyaging across with careless abandon on dark winter evenings—even as they also describe a world flawed and incomplete, of places that have never been and never will be.

And what about all the other maps that we as human beings have created in our efforts to make sense of our experience? What about the empirical maps created by our scientists? Or the temporal maps drawn by our historians? Or the metaphysical maps described by our philosophers? Or the spiritual maps preached by our ministers and rabbis and systematized by our theologians?

Are these maps any different, really, from the nautical charts I learned to love and mistrust as a child? Are any of them to be accepted, uncritically, as statements about what is rather than as propositions about what might be? Are any without error or omission? Are any so carefully wrought as to be able to stand the tests of time and experience without need of revision?

For one with an irreverent cast of mind, the answer to such questions is obvious. Once you've started wondering about maps, once you've started testing, comparing, editing, revising, the need for such a process becomes increasingly apparent and the process itself—for all the maps you use—becomes inevitable. You affirm and you doubt. You accept and you question. You defend and you challenge. You study each new map with all the care and attentiveness you can, and you proceed like a blind person stumbling down a twisted path littered with all manner of dangers and booby traps and dead-ends.

Tonight I sit in my study and unroll a new set of nautical charts that I've just purchased for an upcoming voyage, and I begin the process once more. As the last of the winter light disappears from the window before me, I sail north, relentlessly north, across a fantasy landscape that I suspect may not exist, searching for the bays of next summer.

I wonder what stark and beautiful places I will visit in the coming months. I wonder about their color, their texture, their scale. I wonder what songs the wind will sing in their empty hills and what rhythms the surf will beat against their shores. I wonder what dangers will be hidden in their bays and sounds: both the ones the chart makers have already determined and the ones they have not.

The real voyage begins in June. Just as others that have come before, this one, too, will be an opportunity to encounter the world—not only the world as the chart makers would have us understand it but the world as it actually is. It will be a time for me and the others who sail with me to touch and taste and listen and watch: to gather the evidence of our own senses, the way all sailors must when they journey to a new and unfamiliar coast. It will be a chance for us to test our nautical charts—along with all the other maps our culture has provided to help us make sense of our experience—and to assess for ourselves their truth.

The Ocean Experience

The deep ocean, like the desert, is a setting that is complete and whole without human beings. Most of us may find it difficult to appreciate this statement because most of us, when we encounter the ocean at all, encounter it only at its edges, where the horizon is still just a partial circle and the sea is merely a backdrop for bathing beaches and resort hotels and long promenades of summer houses.

The ocean edges have been transformed by centuries of human presence into places that feel familiar and safe. But the deep ocean is still a wilderness, a place with its own rhythms, its own indecipherable grindings—a place that is not meant (and never was) for creatures like us and where we are, in some mysterious and terrible way, irrelevant.

There is no way to communicate the experience of the deep ocean in words. I've tried—and I've never come close to succeeding. If you want to know this place you have to go there yourself. And go you must without defenses—without the trappings of civilization and its intricate network of social and technological supports. The best way might be to go in a small open boat, without an engine, without any but the basic necessities for survival. If you need a means of locomotion, you might take a set of oars, or you might rig a simple mast and lanteen and hang a few strips of cloth between them, the better to feel the forces of the wind and seas and move in concert with them.

If the open boat seems too sparse a vessel, then maybe you could try a sailboat—something with an enclosed cabin, a bunk to sleep in, a few cupboards for food, a tank full of fresh water. But don't get too much more complicated than this. Keep your vessel simple. For then you may sail for days or weeks or even months, and you may immerse yourself in the ocean's own rhythms, and you may—if you are patient—forget the self you were when you left the land and become something else—something less (and more): a participant.

I have sailed many thousands of miles in the ocean—not always as a participant (this takes time) but sometimes so. There are many who have sailed longer and farther than I—and many who have learned much more. But from time to time I've felt the overwhelming sense of my own inconsequence that this experience evokes and have understood—if only briefly—some of the lessons that are there for human beings to learn.

There are a number of recent propositions about the way the natural world works that appear self-evident from the perspective of the ocean experience. One such proposition has to do with an idea that atmospheric chemist James Lovelock has termed the "Gaia hypothesis"—the idea that the Earth may not simply be an environment for life but may itself be a living, self-sustaining organism.

The longer one sails on the ocean the more plausible this idea becomes. According to the Gaia hypothesis, the world ocean and its complex system of surface and subsurface currents function as a kind of planet-wide circulatory system, transporting heat and chemical substances around the Earth, helping to regulate temperature, precipitation, cloud cover, and other dimensions of global "metabolism." At the same time the atmosphere functions as a sort of protective skin, a living, breathing membrane that shields the organism from space debris and radiation while also trapping heat, regulating surface temperature, releasing unwanted substances to the exosphere. For a sailor who has been immersed in the ocean experience, these and other apparently automatic planetary processes begin to insinuate themselves into consciousness in new and surprising ways. "Gaia" ceases to be some kind of oddball speculation and emerges, instead, as an entirely logical explanation about the way the natural world is connected.

Another proposition that appears self-evident when sailing on the deep ocean centers around an idea that radical environmentalists Bill Devall, George Sessions, and others have termed "deep ecology," the notion that we must dedicate ourselves to sustaining and preserving natural systems independent of their usefulness to human beings. The ocean's wounds can cause a sailor to weep, not for what humanity may have lost in terms of natural beauty or raw materials or food production but for the ocean itself, complete and alone, without regard to people.

It has always struck me as odd to hear certain environmentalists arguing that we need to save the rain forests because of all the miracle pharmaceuticals that we will eventually be able to extract from them—as if the forests' sole purpose were to serve as a chemical warehouse for humankind. The problem with this kind of thinking is that it is really no different than the "competing" view in which the forest represents firewood or building materials or future farmland. Both views rest on the assumption that the ultimate value of the forest lies in its usefulness for humanity. But what about the forest as forest? What about its usefulness for birds and alligators and mosquitoes?

(The irony, of course, is that preserving the forest as forest or the ocean as ocean *is* ultimately critical for humankind. We need the forests and the oceans *as they are* if we are to have a planet that is habitable, not only for fish and birds and monkeys and spiders but for human beings as well.)

There is one other recent proposition—this one more mathematical than scientific—that also appears self-evident when you are sailing on the deep ocean. "Chaos theory" has become its popular name: the study of the apparently random, nonlinear structures that characterize much of our experience.

Since the time of Pythagoras, our mathematical and scientific bias has been to focus our attention on predictable systems, linear functions, patterns with closure. Most of the other "chaotic" patterns in experience have been ignored—mainly because they haven't fit with our mathematical descriptions of reality and we haven't known what to do with them. Then along came a generation of mathematicians equipped with powerful computers that could observe and manipulate the open-ended permutations of nonlinear functions, and chaos theory was born.

Today the study of chaos is at the cutting edge of many fields of scientific and mathematical endeavor—yet from the perspective of the ocean experience, this theory, too, seems childishly apparent. A small boat that is being propelled by the irregular patterns of wind flowing across thousands of square miles of undulating fluid is *surrounded by chaos*. As you watch the clouds, as you stare at the waves, as you follow the flight of birds, as you feel the boat moving underneath you, as you add or shorten sail in response to the dying or the rising of the wind, you are literally swallowed up by nonlinearity, consumed by chaos. There is almost no other kind of reality in the ocean world.

Perhaps it is the sailor in me, but I have always been fascinated by the idea of chaos. One night when I was first reading James Gleick's modern classic on the subject and thinking about the problem of how to understand nonlinear systems, I was suddenly overtaken by an even more immediate problem: hunger. I folded down the corner of the page I was reading (something about a nonlinear pattern called a "fractal structure"), and I walked into the kitchen. On the counter were a pan of leftover spaghetti sauce and a box of number-ten vermicelli. I set the sauce on the stove to simmer. Then I filled a large pot with water, salt, and an ounce of vegetable oil, and I set it on another burner.

Ten minutes later, after the water had come to a rolling boil, I grabbed a fistful of vermicelli and stood with it poised above the pot. Then something stopped me . . . a set of shapes . . . swirling . . . curling . . . spinning . . . defined by the movement of the oil on the surface of the water . . . each shape growing out of the last . . . some large . . . some small . . . all repeating the same basic pattern in endless new combinations.

My god! All of a sudden I realized that in this dynamic interface between liquid and gas I was witnessing the tracing of a fractal structure—the very phenomenon that I had just been reading about. I understood at that moment that chaos was universal. The pattern with no closure, the permutation with no end, the system with no boundary was not just a phenomenon of the ocean experience. It was everywhere—and I felt like throwing off all my clothes and dancing.

The reason human beings feel irrelevant when they sail for many days in the ocean is that out there our linear geometries don't work. Our "rationality" doesn't work. Our systems of cause and effect don't work. Our orderly paradigms of justice and injustice, good and evil, crime and punishment, don't work, either. Like so many other dimensions of our experience, these are contrivances of the solid land that we have devised in an attempt to understand and control the territory in which we live.

For centuries we have been looking for definitive answers, closed systems, gods who explain why—indeed, a creation that has a comprehensible purpose (comprehensible to *us*, that is, whose purpose centers on *us*). In so doing, we have ignored much of what is going on in nature, rationalized the rest, and limited our attention to the parts of our situation that fit, conveniently, into our desire for order and stasis.

Can we stop this searching for simple solutions and this insistence on being at the center of things? Most of the time, it would seem, we cannot. We are too concerned with proving ourselves as agents and doers and makers.

But once in a rare while comes a moment when we are able to stop and feel ourselves dissolve into the progression of the world in time. Such a moment can come, and sometimes does, during the ocean experience—a moment in which we cease to be our "selves," alien and outside, and begin to move with the irregular flow of energy that defines this place and of which we are a part.

Cathedral of the World

Thomas Jefferson once proposed a dramatic equation: "My mind is my church." His proposition has been remembered, I think, because it incorporates so perfectly the basic tenets of eighteenth-century rationalism, the politics of democracy, and the emerging cult of the individual. In five short words Jefferson was able to articulate his belief in the preeminence of the intellect and the objectivity of knowledge and to give voice to the hope of young America.

I have been tempted by Jefferson's phrase—as thousands of others in the generations after him have also been tempted. When I was a young man I was often willing to repeat his words as my own, buoyed by their optimism and encouraged by their almost childlike affirmation of the visibility and accessibility of truth.

Just as Jefferson, I was convinced that the church of my youth was full of hocus-pocus. Some of the teachings I encountered there seemed the perpetuation of empty phrases. Some seemed the repetition of rituals no longer understood. And some seemed actually wrong—perhaps even destructive—as they attempted to divide the people of the Earth into those who were the favored "children" of a petulant and possessive god and those who were not.

It seemed to me then that there must be more to the truth than what I was hearing from the pulpit. "My mind is my church" seemed to make better sense. At least it left a way for each person to move beyond the rote phrases and inconsistencies of an ancient credo and to seek a deity more suited to the dictates of his own time and experience.

But there is more to the mind and more to the processes of human cognition than Jefferson ever dreamed. More, too, than I suspected in my own naive enthusiasm over Jefferson's phrase. Jefferson lived at the beginning of the age of science, and his celebration of the mind is also a celebration of the scientific worldview. But we live in a generation after Freud and Adler and Jung, a generation sensitized to the turmoils of the mind. Our science still celebrates the mind as a rational instrument—but it also warns of the mind's dark underside: a place of shadows and nightmares and irrational fears, a festering, weed-filled maze in which we can lose ourselves just as easily, sometimes, as we can discover the paths of truth.

But if the ancient rituals and insular worldviews of traditional religion can constitute one kind of dead-end and the dark convolutions of the mind can constitute another, then where does a person turn? Where is the path and what is the shape of the truth we seek, and how will we recognize it when we encounter it, face to face?

One answer to such a question—the one that has come to seem most appropriate to me—is simple. Turn to the world. Seek the experience of unadorned nature. Search for what's left of wilderness, before it has been permanently altered by the tampering of humankind. Open your mind and senses to the dynamic shapes and rhythms of the Earth. Try to comprehend what the natural world has to teach—not to impose patterns of your own but to respond to the patterns that arise from everywhere around you.

The immediate difficulty in accomplishing such a task centers upon the fundamental workings of human cognition. As creatures of culture, we necessarily perceive by means of the intellectual, ethical, and spiritual paradigms or "maps" that we learn from our elders and carry around with us. A child without language, for instance, might look upon nature and perceive only confusion. A Pentecostal Christian might look upon nature and perceive the hand of God. A scientist might look upon nature and perceive the laws of thermodynamics or the elaborate workings of biochemical processes.

How can we experience the world for what it *is* and not for what we choose to make of it? Maybe the answer is that we cannot. Maybe we are—all of us—trapped inside a series of perceptual feedback loops—doomed to circle forever within the confines of our own cognitive apparatus so that we may only see and comprehend what we have been preconditioned to see and comprehend.

Or maybe—just maybe—there is a breakaway point—some level of encounter with the natural world in which the experience itself provides the paradigm and we learn a new way of bringing it into our awareness.

What is a cathedral, after all, but a place to go as we seek to understand how the cosmos works and what our proper place is in it? Over the centuries, cathedrals have been built to guide our minds and spirits upward "toward God," to inspire, to overwhelm, to cause us to feel humble and small. But the stone and mortar cathedrals of traditional religion have been propagandistic—which is to say, they've been built to guide us toward a preconceived notion of the truth—one that is immersed in human politics and entangled in the perpetuation of human institutions.

Maybe the time has come to look to another kind of cathedral—not inward to Jefferson's "church of the mind," as this may prove a dark and convoluted place, but outward to a grander, more awe-inspiring, and far more objective structure: a cathedral of the world.

Here, if we can silence our egos for a moment and set aside our preconceptions about who we think we are, we may begin to perceive some of the lessons that the rest of nature has to teach: lessons not of personality but of relationship, not of order but of complexity, not of private property but of shared responsibility, not of rationality but of mystery, not of the ultimacy of the human enterprise but of the interdependency of all life.

The Flight of Seabirds

There is a common misconception among landspeople that the surface of the ocean is a blank, unpopulated wasteland. I understand this misconception. I've had the same flawed impression of the desert as I've driven across its flat brown miles in a car. I am not a desert person. I've never learned how to differentiate among the russets and umbers and raw siennas of the desert landscape in order to discern the profusion of crawling things that populate the dust. But I've sat for a thousand hours at sea at the helm of a sailboat, climbing azure water-mountains, slipping into the purple canyons of troughs, staring at the watery terrain and learning, often without intending, how to observe and eventually to comprehend the maze of biomass that ranges across its surface.

The seabirds are the most obvious inhabitants of this place. Beaked and clawed and winged like feathered reptiles, they have evolved out of an entirely different family of living creatures than the human beings that sail here. But they share the air with us—which makes them accessible to our senses in a way that our closer relatives, the whales and dolphins, seldom are.

There are three types of birds that one encounters at sea. First are the land birds, who cross the open water only when required on their long migratory journeys. Next are the gulls and terns—partial residents of this place—who fish the sea fringes by day but return to their nesting islands every night. And finally are the pelagic birds, the wanderers, who live along the surface of the sea like fishes of the air, and for whom the ocean is home.

The land birds are wind swimmers that fly by pumping their wings. When they cross a stretch of open water during a long migration, they move like tunneled, driven creatures whose whole being seems focused into a predetermined destination. If they are blown off course or carried by a storm too far away from the land, they risk dehydration and eventual exhaustion. Then they have no choice but to continue their struggle—pumping, pumping, pumping, until their strength fails and they finally tumble into the water and drown.

Seagulls and terns also fly from time to time by pumping their wings—because, in truth, they are only partly seabirds. In the morning when they leave their rookery islands they often travel in straight lines, swimming against the wind like finches or blackbirds, heading out to the fishing grounds where they will spend the day. Once they are properly at sea they seem to relax, as if they've just remembered what a pleasure it is to be free of the land. At these times they resemble the pelagic birds, gliding and banking and diving for food. But as dusk approaches, they mount the wind again and turn resolutely homeward, pumping their wings and racing the sun toward shore.

The only true seabirds are the ocean wanderers: the albatrosses and fulmars, the shearwaters and skuas and petrels. These birds roam the waves, sometimes for years on end, only returning to the land for brief periods of nesting and raising their young. During all the rest of their lives they remain at sea, following routes that are poorly understood by human observers, traveling as wind sailors across untold thousands of miles.

Out in the ocean these birds are a mariner's constant companions. Along with the surface of the sea, they are what he watches. Their movement is mesmerizing. The patterns they trace across the surface of the water seem at once random and oddly predictable. In the daytime they rise from behind a breaking crest, bank into a stall, tip, dive, run down the belly of a trough, disappear behind the curl of the next crest. At night they chatter in the dark as their shadows dart in and out of the circles of the ship's running lights.

Many times when I've been at sea and watching the birds, I've found myself wondering about the mystery of their flight. How do these creatures, which are heavier than the air, conspire to leave the surface of the water? How do they rise without apparent effort into an invisible medium? How do they move against the flow of wind when common sense suggests that they should be pushed in the opposite direction?

The answer that any good engineer will give to questions like these has to do with the aerodynamics of an airfoil—a complex shape that occurs most perfectly in nature in the wings of soaring birds. This is the same shape that men in this century have learned to use for the construction of aircraft wings, the same shape that some nameless mariner stumbled upon three thousand years ago for use in fashioning the vertical wings of sailboats.

I know about airfoils. I've read the scientific explanation of how they work dozens of times. I've repeated this explanation to novice sailors on countless occasions.

There is a diagram that appears in encyclopedias and flight manuals and sailing primers of an airfoil shape—a pair of lines flat on the bottom and curved on the top, with a series of vectors in the form of small arrows that represent the flow of the air as it moves along the two surfaces. The diagram looks like this:

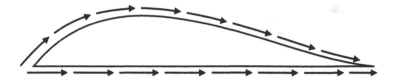

According to aerodynamic theory, an airfoil works on the principle of lift: a force created by a pressure differential in the stream of air flowing past the foil. Because one of the foil's surfaces is curved and the other is straight, the air molecules that pass over them must travel unequal distances. The molecules that pass along the longer, curved surface must accelerate in order to keep up with the molecules that pass along the shorter, straight surface. As this acceleration occurs, the upper molecules spread apart, reducing their density and creating an area of relative low pressure. Meanwhile, the molecules on the flat surface are left with a positive pressure, so that they push upward against the area of low pressure, forcing the wing to rise.

Fine . . . just so. Now I understand the symbols in

the diagram and I know, operationally, how an airfoil works. But does this knowledge bring me any closer to an understanding of the mystery of flight or to an appreciation of its beauty?

The answer is no—and the reason has to do with a fundamental incongruity between a complex phenomenon in nature and its scientific description. The problem with the diagrammatic rendering of an airfoil is that it is too fractured, too mechanical. It is a clever explanation of the interplay of forces at work on a physical object, but it captures nothing of the flow and feel of the thing it tries to describe. Like attempting to teach a novice sailor how to make a boat move to windward by issuing a series of verbal instructions, the scientific description of an airfoil fragmentizes an experience that is fluid. It tries to translate into words and symbols something that is—in the end—ineffable.

Watching seabirds tip and glide across the wake of a sailboat far out at sea has become, for me, a kind of avian magic show. The ease and grace of the birds' movements as they soar fractions of inches above the waves is like a sleight of hand performed by a troupe of master magicians—a dare repeated over and over again, challenging the audience to guess how the trick is done. Aerodynamic formulas and diagrams of airfoils notwithstanding, the magicians win the dare every time. Their flight remains a dazzling aerobatic display—and the dexterity of their wingtips makes our own much-vaunted fingers and op-posing thumbs seem crude in comparison.

In the end, the birds serve as a point of contact with the ocean world. Their effortless movement speaks of their near-perfect adaptation to their natural setting. Their apparent aimlessness evokes a spirit of freedom that is worthy, if not always of our emulation, then at least of our wonder. And the careless ease with which they fly posits them as unself-conscious celebrants of their ocean world, appearing to all the rest of nature to be flying for the pure joy of it.

In the winter of 1982 a flatbed eighteen-wheeler arrived in the backyard of my family's house in Maryland to deliver the unfinished hull and deck of a sailboat that would eventually be named Brendan's Isle. *The boat-building project that followed lasted eighteen months and required six-thousand hours to complete. The work was long and full of surprises. Each day, however, always began the same . . .*

The Tunnel

"Morning, John."

"Morning, Skipper."

Light a pipe. Fill a mug from the automatic coffeemaker in the corner. Inspect the edges of the chisels, the handsaws, the table saw, the radial saw. Oil the metal surfaces of the power tools. Tension the band-saw blade.

"I'll sharpen the plane irons, Skipper."

"Okay, John. I'll light the heater on the boat."

Open the doorway that leads from the basement

shop in the back of the house to the long plastic-covered shed. This is a makeshift workspace constructed of pine two-by-sixes bolted together into a series of eight stations, each seven feet apart and spanning a width of twenty feet. A double layer of translucent plastic is battened over the roof to keep the snow and rain out. A single layer is fastened to the sides.

The boat sits in the shed like a great white leviathan, frozen and motionless. It fills the covered space from edge to edge and end to end, its keel resting on railroad ties and its hull cradled in four pairs of patent stands positioned at ten-foot intervals and tuned together with tensioning chains.

Move carefully around the perimeter of the stands. Climb the twenty-two steps to the deck. Step over the gunwale and around the deckhouse, ducking under the trusses on the shed roof. Slide back the companionway hatch and climb down six steps into the hull. In December when the job began there was nothing inside but a rough plywood floor and half a dozen plywood bulkheads. The hull was an empty tube fifty feet long and fourteen feet wide. The dark blue inner surface of the hull, the gray overhead, the paint-spattered floor defined the boundaries of the space. The tunnel, we called it.

The tunnel was a place we started to work, John and Kay and I. It was an ever-present physical reminder of a task that seemed, to me at least, the most difficult thing I had ever set out to do. One day soon after the boat arrived, I climbed the steps and sat alone, staring at the empty space around me and trying to imagine how I would ever find the energy to begin. I sat with my eyes closed and my face in my hands, and I came dangerously close to crying. I thought I might have made the most terrible mistake of my life.

The tunnel began as a question in a language I didn't understand. But now, as the construction proceeds, there is change visible. Not always day to day, but week to week and month to month the tunnel is transformed. Now it is a chain locker, a toilet compartment, a pair of tandem cabins, a galley, an aft cabin.

Bulkheads are fared out with plastic body-filler, doors are cut into the plywood, headers are installed, Formica sheets are glued onto the plywood, bunks are fiberglassed to the hull, mahogany furniture is assembled in the shop and fastened into place. The furniture expands and defines the space and makes it comprehensible.

The tunnel began as a physical space. It has evolved into a state of mind. The tunnel is comfortable now: a job to do, a new skill to practice, a place to be alone. It is a way of centering. An hour, a week, a month are unimportant here. The only matter of importance is the task at hand. All time in the tunnel is present-time.

In the center of the boat there is a large area over

fourteen feet square, eventually to become the main sa-loon. Until we are ready to build this area, it will serve as an onboard workshop. A fluorescent light hangs tempo-rarily on nails spiked into one of the structural bulk-heads. A tool bench, a portable band saw, and a kerosene heater fill the rest of the space. The heater will raise the temperature inside the boat to near sixty degrees in an-other hour. Meanwhile, if the day is sunny, the green-house effect under the plastic shed will heat the decks into the seventies by noon, even on the coldest days.

Once the heater is started I return to the shop. John is already working on a piece of mahogany fascia that we templated yesterday. He asks me to prepare the edges with a plane while he drills and cuts the dowel. After the fascia is glued, we take twenty minutes for a cup of tea (John) and coffee (me), and we talk about the rest of the day.

John is a man without boundaries. He used to race bicycles when he was a young man. He climbed most of the major mountains of western Europe before he was twenty-three. He is a mechanic, a structural engineer, a charter boat skipper, a world-class sailor with fifty thou-sand miles and three Atlantic crossings in his own boats. He is also a master shipwright, trained in the shipyards of northwest England during the era of the great Atlantic passenger liners.

One day as we are hand-cutting dovetails for a stack

of drawers, John tells me about his teacher in the wood shops of Cheshire and Lancashire, a man he calls Old Benbow. He flashes a self-conscious grin as he thinks about how "old" Old Benbow was—probably forty-five or fifty. John is fifty-two. I am the apprentice now, and John is the master. "Old John," I call him.

Each of the stories John tells about himself is set in the context of a job we do together: planing a stack of cypress boards, installing a teak step, designing a door-way, routering several hundred shiplap panels. We are fortunate. We have the luxury of weeks and months without interruption, with plenty of time for talking. John's stories evolve carelessly, in random associations that do not require a beginning or middle or end. Yet finally, like the weave of an intricate cloth, the stories fit together to form the chronicle of a life.

In the afternoons Kay comes down to the shop to work. She has sailed a hundred difficult passages with me in the twenty-three years of our marriage, but none has ever been as long or difficult as this one. In all the weeks and months that I've been living in the tunnel, she has kept the rest of our lives from flying apart. Every day after the meals and shopping and cleaning are done, she comes to the basement ready for whatever job there is for her to do. She doesn't complain, even when the work is tedious. She sands twenty raised-panel cupboard doors—

all by hand. She cuts a thousand mahogany plugs on the drill press, rough sands three hundred running feet of shiplap panel, mixes the glue for a new piece of fascia, cuts a dozen handholds on the band saw.

Eight months ago I had been paralyzed by indecision. Kay was the one then who understood the importance of this undertaking for me—for us. She was the one who urged me to sell my old schooner, then to call the designer of the new boat in Seattle and order the hull and deck. If it hadn't been for her encouragement at the beginning, the project would never have started. And now she has the hardest job of all. Twenty-four hours a day, she must live with someone who is living in the tunnel. It is a job that requires infinite patience and love.

What is to be gained from this self-imposed retreat into a tiny world fifty feet long and fourteen feet wide, filled with the smells of wood chips and sawdust and glue? Two important things, I think. The first is an intimacy with the boat. Every component we build grows as an extension of our own experience. Month by month a blueprint evolves in our minds—and it will remain there, so that some day on a lonely sea or in a remote foreign port we will know this boat in the same way that a parent knows his own child. This is a knowledge for which we are willing to disrupt our lives—a knowledge that may one day save our lives.

The second thing to be gained is more difficult to describe. It has to do with sharpening tools, selecting the correct grain, thinking in three dimensions, templating, building by eye. It has to do with techniques: rabbit, miter, scarphe, dovetail, halflap, shiplap, butt, spline. It has to do with tools: chisels, gouges, bullnose and panel and jack planes, bevel, marking gauge, wing dividers, compass. Each technique and each tool enables a skill. Together they form a repertoire.

John is the master and Kay and I are his apprentices, but we are doing more than building a boat. We are also learning an ancient and demanding discipline. Many years ago I studied as a graduate student at two distinguished universities, but neither of the disciplines I learned then compares in breadth or intensity with the one we learn week by week and month by month in this backyard boat shop.

By late afternoon the winter sun drops behind the corner of the house and the temperature in the shed falls quickly. The darkness grows inside the boat. I extinguish the cabin heater and snap on the bulb that hangs on one of the roof trusses over the cockpit.

This is a moment of the day I have come to look forward to—a time to stop and dream. I set my tools down and slide around the cockpit bench to sit behind the empty steering station. I close my eyes, and for an instant I feel the boat as I imagine she will be some day, charging to windward into a short chop with the spray driving in sheets across the foredeck, or rolling down long Atlantic hills with the headsails poled out wing and wing.

I feel like celebrating this evening. The job is so long and we have come so far. Today we've completed three thousand hours, halfway to our goal of launch by July. John returns to the boat looking for a tool, and I ask him to sit and share a moment of self-congratulation. When he declines to join me, I become annoyed.

"Three thousand hours—doesn't that fact count for anything with you?"

"The bunk boards still need cutting out," John says.

"Dammit, man, you're not listening to me. Think now. When you used to climb those mountains in Europe and you finally got to the top of one, didn't you ever stop—just for a few minutes—to enjoy the feeling of accomplishment?"

John screws up his face and stares at me, as if he cannot understand my question. "I was always too worried about how I was going to get back down," he says.

Now I am the one who stares at him, for I cannot understand his answer.

I won't understand it either, until long after this boat is finished, until she's sailed more than sixty thousand miles and crossed two oceans. Only then will I begin to comprehend what all these months have been about. They are not about accomplishing some arbitrary goal—not about "arriving" anywhere at all—but only about the intricacies and challenges of getting there.

The present: . . . catch it if you can.
    —Annie Dillard, *Pilgrim at Tinker Creek*

On Living in the Present

What does it mean to live in the present—with your mind, your senses, all of your awareness tuned to the same frequency? What does it mean to see the textures in a leaf? To watch the turbulence roil on the surface of a cloud? To feel the pressure of the wind on your skin? To hear the nuances of a melody as it is plucked, note by note, on the strings of an instrument? Poets have asked this question. Philosophers have asked it. Mystics have dreamed visions about it. Ascetics have suffered on beds of nails in search of answers.

Is living in the present simply a matter of confronting events as they occur in time and living without carryover, as John and Kay and I were sometimes able to do while building *Brendan's Isle*? Is it a means of dedicating oneself to simplicity, as certain old Quakers would have it? Is it a formula for celebrating life, as Mike the Hermit explains in Wylie Blanchet's *The Curve of Time*? Or is it more than all of these? Is it, perhaps, something akin to Annie Dillard's "state of innocence"—a situation she describes in *Pilgrim at Tinker Creek* as "the spirit's unself-conscious state at any moment of pure devotion to any object"?

I have been moved by Dillard's speculations about living in the present—even as I've also been confused by her sometimes tiered and convoluted language. She uses words with strong religious connotations ("the spirit's . . . pure devotion . . .") to describe a state of unfiltered awareness that is utterly physical and sensory. Yet at the same time she describes the state as "unselfconscious," keying on what I would agree to be the single most important quality of this experience.

Ego, as in so many dimensions of our being, is the culprit, obscuring the present and clouding our ability to perceive what is before us. The present is accessible only when we have forgotten our "selves," when we have escaped (or been released) from memory and desire. To really see a cloud, to feel the sun on the nape of your neck, to hear the crash of breaking waves, to smell the perfumes of the forest at night—to experience any of these things for exactly what each is—we must somehow disconnect from the background static of our own projections, desires, interior voices. We must become, for an instant, pure receptors. Our minds must free themselves from the fetters of our "selves" and *connect directly*, imprinting only what is, without nostalgia or hope.

There is mystery in all of this. Perhaps this is why it is so hard to speak or write about. Lord knows, it is hard enough to *do*, this matter of instantaneous connecting with an object, of living entirely in the present.

It happens sometimes when you sail. Not all the time—not even most of the time—but sometimes. And that is more than I can say for almost any other setting or activity that I customarily find myself involved in.

There are three reasons, I think, for why it happens here. First is the real-time quality of the enterprise. Sailing forces you to focus, to pay attention to the events and objects around you: the wind, the sky, the surface of the sea, the pressures on the helm, the noises and movements of the boat. If you want to be able to sail, you must be exactly where you are and nowhere else.

The second reason is the absence of extraneous clutter. There are no telephones nearby when you are sailing. No newspapers or television sets. No unexpected guests dropping by for a visit. Even if you have other shipmates, the division of labor on a small boat is such that there are many hours when you are on your own, required to function in a kind of enforced solitude in which the sensory world is all there is and you must learn to cope.

The third and probably the most important reason is the feeling, as you move with (and are moved by) the boat, that you are not really in control here—that "you," as ego, are not even very important within the web of forces that surround you. It is this last ingredient, I suspect, that completes the equation. The sailor is not really the one who sails the boat. In fact, in a very real sense, it is the boat that sails the sailor. Any good sailor will tell you this. The trick is to let go. To let the boat lead in the dance. To become the partner, the medium through which the boat is sailed.

Not all sailors are equally good at this letting go. I sailed once on a long summer voyage with a young crew member—let's call her Ellen—who exhibited a kind of brute force approach to sailing. Ellen was strong—too strong—and she was always tying a knot too tight or over-winding a winch or steering a serpentine course that had nothing to do with the way the boat wanted to go. For three long months she was so intent on making things happen through sheer force of will that she could never simply be where she was and tune in to the events that were taking place around her.

At the other end of the spectrum was Susan, a novice who had never been to sea until she sailed off into the ocean one blustery June morning with her husband and Kay and me. For the first half day she struggled, unable to get the feel of the boat. As the wind rose, she slalomed across the faces of mounting seas, coming dangerously close to losing control and broaching. And then something happened. The boat steadied out. The hull and rudder settled into a contented hum, and the boat's wake became straight and true. Susan looked up from the helm with a little half-smile. "I've got it," she said. "It's just like centering a pot."

I am not a potter, as Susan is, and I've never tried to center a lump of clay on a turning wheel. So I can't say for sure why her metaphor worked. All I know is that it *did* work—which must mean that, like sailing, centering a pot requires an unself-conscious moment—a moment in which the "I" of the potter disappears and there is only the clay, the turning wheel, the intuitive center.

After that epiphany Susan became a sailor. The size of the seas increased all day, the wind accelerated into a clear air gale, and, with Susan at the helm, the boat surfed down the faces of waves with never a contrary swagger. Susan-the-potter withdrew into the background—and in her place appeared an unself-conscious sailor, focused on the spectacle of indigo troughs and turquoise crests, centered on the surging and plunging of the hull, and living—for this moment—in the present.

In early summer 1984, soon after she was finished building, Brendan's Isle *and a crew of five departed from the U.S. East Coast headed toward a mountainous archipelago three hundred miles east of Iceland: the Faroe Islands. Just over three weeks later she was struggling toward landfall in gale force winds and storm seas, and I was nearing the accomplishment of a goal that I had dreamed about for decades: a high-latitude crossing of the North Atlantic under sail.*

Day Twenty-Two

Moments ago, sitting at the chart table next to my watchmate Kell, I stared at the final terse phrase of his four-hour summary as he entered it in the navigator's log: "howling and wet." Kell scribbled the words in a nearly unreadable scrawl, closed the logbook, and moved forward into his bunk. Now I, too, retreat to my own bunk. I lie on my back, elbows and knees jammed against stacks of pillows and dirty clothing to keep myself from being thrown about, and I think about the inadequacy of

Kell's words—hell, the inadequacy of *any* words—to describe the experience of sailing in a full gale at sixty-one degrees north latitude in the open Atlantic.

How many accounts of small boat voyages have been written, how many actual sailing logs have been strewn with the same kinds of terse, inadequate phrases? When you've read enough of such accounts, you begin to fill the spaces between the words. You compose your own string of hyperboles and build them into fantasies of exploding seas, groaning, overstressed rigging, unthinkable noise.

I smile inwardly in the rising light of a subarctic morning. Not true. There simply are no words, neither the real ones nor the imagined ones, to communicate the immediacy of this moment. It *is* howling and wet out there—no arguing that. But at least now, in the relative quiet of the cabins, there is also an odd feeling of peace, as if this improbable place and time are exactly as they should be, as if the gale and the boat and the five who sail her belong together here.

Brendan's Isle is a strong sea boat. If any of our crew had harbored secret doubts before about her abilities, they've been put to rest in the last eight days of gale force winds. Even here, in the downside bunk of the aft cabin, I can feel that she is moving well. She carries a triple-reefed mainsail and a small, heavy storm jib flown from an intermediate stay well aft of the bows. Kell and I have been taking turns at the helm since midnight, steering across seas that have the boat caroming from side to side like a bobsled. We are both happy to be out of the weather for a few hours while the next watch freezes their fingers and toes up there. We are both tired and a bit numb in the brain. But I suspect we are also both about as high as we've ever been in our lives.

I pull my knees into a fetal tuck under the sleeping bag and jam my hands into my armpits for warmth. I am too excited right now for sleep. The sounds and motion down here are familiar after twenty-two days at sea, but I listen as if each sensation were happening for the first time. I listen to the rumble of waves moving along the hull, the creak of the steering cable in the lazarette astern, the thunder of drawers and cupboard doors crashing together as the boat lurches forward. Overhead, I listen to the hiss of deckhouse ports as green water runs past, followed by the gasp and swirl of scupper drains struggling to clear before another wall of water tumbles along the decks to fill them again.

A shudder runs the length of the boat, and I'm thrown hard against my elbow. The two hull lites next to my bunk dip under water and remain that way for what seems an excessively long time. I listen for a call from the deck, and when I don't hear one, I become uneasy. Mike and Andrew are on watch for the next four hours, and I know from experience that neither is inclined to shorten sail when the wind goes up a notch. Hell, I think, I want to get to the Faroe Islands as badly as they do—but I'd like to have as much as possible of the rigging and sails intact when we get there. I'm about to roll out of my bunk and climb to the cockpit to announce my annoyance when the hull ports finally emerge from the water and the boat seems to regain her old motion.

Let it go, I tell myself. They're doing fine up there. Close your eyes and take a long, deep breath. Let it go and enjoy the ride.

I lie as still as I can and try to drink in the sensations of tumbling headlong into the final day. Yes, I'm excited—wound up like a coil of spring steel. But now there is another feeling that also rises into consciousness—an odd sort of sadness. Perhaps I *don't* really want to get to the Faroe Islands as badly as the others do. Or perhaps, in a strange way, none of us wants to get there. At least not so soon, after all that has happened to bring us to this point.

I think of the hours of standing watch on deck, the shifting colors of sea and sky, the sounds of the wind, the whine and shudder of the hull as it accelerates down the faces of waves. I think of the undulating shapes of the horizon in the rising dawn, the shadows of pilot whales buried in a following sea, the dorsal fins of hammerheads so close to the hull they seem to touch, the circle of light around the moon before an approaching storm.

I think of an evening somewhere weeks ago—or was

it yesterday?—a quiet night in the Gulf Stream. Kell and I had just gone forward to change a headsail in the dropping breeze. Suddenly the water on either side of the bows erupted in tunnels of phosphorescence, like rocket trails in an inverted sky. Below, a herd of dolphin played just under the cutwater, creating one of the strangest phenomena to be found in this strange ocean world: bioluminescence. We had both seen the same display often as it flashed in the turbulence of the boat's wake, but we had never seen it like this, buried half a dozen feet beneath the black surface of the sea, crisscrossing in blue-green trails of liquid light. Kell and I forgot the task that had brought us forward and watched with a kind of stupid fascination.

Clock time means almost nothing out here, and we live instead in a much more immediate and primitive realm of event time. An hour is distorted into a month by the brilliance of the moon or the onset of a line of thunder squalls (or the luminescence of dolphin trails under the bows). Meanwhile a day, two days, a week dissolve into a chaos of momentary impressions: the crack of flogging sails, the cry of seabirds in the night, the smell of cooking food.

I think about the relentless pleasure of those galley smells—hot coffee, cranberry bread, fried sausage, onions simmering in a beef stock stew, cocoa, curry and rice, red cabbage and sour cream, split-pea soup. One stormy night as *Brendan* tumbles headlong into crossing seas, Andrew decides to serve his turn as dinner cook dressed in a floppy blue lumber jacket, oversized gray flannel trousers, and bright red suspenders. He looks like some kind of circus clown as he moves in an exaggerated crouch, lurching from counter to sink to stove in a valiant attempt to keep himself from being thrown across the galley.

Pots and pans tumble across slick surfaces. A carton of milk spills onto the floor. An open box of rice falls into the cupboard behind the stove. Instead of spewing forth a string of angry oaths, however, the clown-cook skates across the mess on a dish towel juggling a stick of butter and two packages of frozen asparagus and singing at the top of his lungs. In his enthusiasm for the task at hand, he exhibits the same spirit that has infected this crew for three and a half thousand miles, and soon he is filling the cabins to overflowing with the smells of mid-Atlantic feasting about to begin.

The following morning under an ominous sky, Kell spots the sail of an approaching vessel. He tries to make contact, first on the VHF radio, then by climbing to the top of *Brendan*'s deckhouse and waving his arms. At its closest approach the vessel passes several long seas away. Only the top of its mast is visible when both boats are buried in a trough, but when they climb to a crest, the rest of the rig and all three hulls appear: a cluster of dark forms that identify the visitor as a racing trimaran, almost certainly one of the hundred or so competitors sailing from Plymouth to Newport in this year's single-handed OSTAR race.

There is no response to Kell's radio call and no answer to his hail. The solo voyager must be asleep, trusting to chance that there will be no logs or basking whales or other vessels in his path. Both boats are traveling fast, and their combined speeds separate them as quickly as they have come together. Kell loses sight of the hulls in less than a minute and the rig and mast soon afterward. *Brendan* is alone again in these endless hills of the North Atlantic and will not encounter another sign of human life for sixteen hundred miles.

Solitude is one of the essential commodities that each of us has come out here to find. Our momentary friend on the trimaran has guaranteed the success of his search by sailing alone. Here aboard *Brendan's Isle* we have the companionship of a watchmate or the society of an entire crew at meals to break the lonely hours of solo watch or rest time in the bunk. But solitude is more than mere physical separation from others. It is an attitude, a condition of the spirit, a meditative distance from the clutter of life ashore. Here, even in the company of shipmates, there are few interruptions. The scale of events is gigantic. The pressure of each moment fills the senses and clears the brain of that maze of irrelevancies that is such a familiar backdrop to most of the rest of our lives.

One of my teachers many years ago had been formally educated in the West but born and raised as an Indian Buddhist. Several of the strange images of his language come back to me now as I lie in the solitude of this final morning at sea. To most of his students, this odd little man spoke in riddles that seemed to defy the sort of logic we had all grown up to accept as truth. When he spoke of the world and how it worked, he used an ancient Sanskrit word: *pratityasamutpada.* Roughly translated, it means something like "the interdependency and interconnectiveness of all things." I went one day to his office to ask about an assignment, but our conversation soon turned to this idea of interconnectiveness. I couldn't get it, I admitted—couldn't even pronounce the word. As a member in good standing of the Western scientific tradition, I was hooked on the opposite idea of *differentiation* as the key to understanding the world. We need to observe, measure, organize our impressions into class, phylum, order, family, genus, species. Darwin, not Buddha, was the guru who would help us make sense out of the puzzle.

The teacher answered my outburst with silence. He sat quietly for almost a minute, then gestured toward a patch of grass outside his window. It was viridian green in the sunlight. He gestured toward a branch of yellow

leaves—then, randomly, toward an empty metal hook behind the office door, a porcelain figure on his desk, his
own reflection in the window glass, a small bird on the
roof outside, a patch of sky. As he pointed, he let the
silence last too long, and then he smiled. "Now do you
understand?" he said, as if to resolve once and for all my
sophomoric misconception.

The odd thing is that even though at the time I
didn't understand at all, I remember his charade with a
particular vividness. There was something else he felt and
somehow communicated—a kind of joyousness—that ac-
companied his silence. Now, after the solitude of twenty-
two days at sea, I wonder if each of us on this boat may be
feeling a similar joyousness.

I imagine myself sitting with my shipmates up in the
cockpit in the midst of this gale, gesturing the way that
odd little man once did. I point to the streams of spindrift
that intersect our wake, the flashes of silver at the top of
each sea, the spring-tight rigging wire, the broken lines of
cloud at the horizon, the gray fulmar that glides along a
trough without moving its wings, the reflection of my own
orange parka in the binnacle cover, the triangular patch
of jib. I wait until the rhythm of the gale and the sea and
the boat become a silence, and then I smile and mutter,
"Now do you understand?"

The boat lurches again. The drawers and cupboards
thunder in a drumroll and I'm picked up bodily from my

bunk and dropped against the cabin side. The two hull lites next to me bury themselves under water once more, and I recall with a certain detached amusement that these are the only two lites in the boat that were still leaking when we left the Chesapeake Bay. If this motion continues much longer, my bunk mattress will fill with cold seawater, and all this mass of clothing and pillows and sleeping bags will begin to feel like a bundle of cold compresses.

No matter. If we maintain anything close to our present speed, this afternoon will be time to hang every soggy bag and mattress and every pile of old mildewed clothing out in the sunlight of a sheltered fiord somewhere in the Faroe Islands. And how will I feel then? Elated, perhaps? Or still vaguely disappointed that the voyage must come so suddenly to an end?

I roll onto my side, prop my back against a stack of pillows, and concentrate on the rhythm of the boat as it shudders and falls against crossing seas. The noise fades slowly into a lullaby, and I pull the bag up over my eyes, waiting for sleep.

Encounters with Leviathans

Why have so many of our present generation become so fascinated with watching the great whales, with chasing after them in converted fishing trawlers and photographing their acrobatics from the decks of eco-tour boats? Is our sudden attentiveness an expression of some kind of collective remorse for having hunted these creatures to the brink of extinction? Or is it something else: a yearning for primal contact, a quest for evolutionary roots, a fascination with size and brute strength and freakishness in nature?

As a sailor I've encountered the great whales at sea many times. The first time was when I was a small child, sailing with my parents along the coast of Maine. The creature we met that day was a giant blue whale, lacerated with the aftermath of a long and dangerous life at sea. The whale was basking in a lazy swell, seemingly unaware of our approach, and we almost sailed up on his back (adding yet another scar to the collection already present) before my father spotted him and veered away.

Since then there have been many other meetings, some in the company of whale-watching boats near the coasts of Long Island or Massachusetts or Nova Scotia, some in the solutude of a deep ocean passage a thousand miles from the nearest land.

One of the most dramatic encounters I can recall happened during a recent summer voyage with a group of sail-trainees aboard *Brendan's Isle*. We were sailing that evening in the southern approaches to the Gulf of St. Lawrence. Twenty miles to the west rose the highlands of Cape Breton. Ten miles directly ahead loomed the jagged cliffs of St. Paul Island, crowned with an intermittent pulse of light from a lighthouse that marked its western end. Between the two areas of land an orange circle of sun hovered a few degrees above the edge of the sea, measuring the northern sunset with shadows that stretched away from the boat almost to the opposite horizon.

In the dropping light, one of my young crew made a discovery that eventually brought everyone else on deck. At first she was not sure what she saw—only that it seemed to be something dark moving in the water a few hundred yards astern. Then she heard a blow—long and deep—and another—and she realized that she had somehow sailed *Brendan's Isle* into the center of a large pod of fin whales.

Because of their streamlined proportions and the fast speeds they are able to travel through the water, fin whales have sometimes been called the greyhounds of the sea. Adult finnies can sustain speeds of twenty knots and more and may grow to eighty feet in length and weigh as much as fifty tons. Yet when they swim, they show only a tiny dorsal fin and a small section of back—no head, no flundering tail. The dramatic part of an encounter with fin whales is thus not what you see but what you hear: the blow. It begins with an exhale like a giant bellows, followed by the sharp, sucking sound of inhale. Above the sound comes a geyser of mist that hangs in the still air like a small cloud for a minute or more, marking the place where the whale has been.

That night near St. Paul Island our helmsperson stood quietly behind the wheel while the others on the crew arranged themselves around her in the cockpit.

Each time a whale blew, one of us pointed in silence toward the spot where the mist cloud hovered above the water, and the helmsperson adjusted her course. In this way we approached the pod of finnies closer and closer as the darkness dropped around us.

Should we have been afraid? I'm not sure. Over the years I've learned not to be. Partly because in literally hundreds of encounters, I've never witnessed an aggressive act by any of the great whales. These fin whales were much larger than our boat, far more maneuverable, many times faster. They were better adapted to every condition out here, and we had no chance of outrunning them if any had suddenly decided to turn and attack. We were the vulnerable party in this encounter—we were the intruders—while they were at home.

During meetings such as this I've often wondered why these gigantic creatures exercise such restraint when it comes to acts of retaliation against our species—especially in light of the history of our relationship with them over the last several centuries. Our slaughter of the great whales began on this side of the Atlantic in the Gulf of St. Lawrence perhaps as many as five hundred years ago. The first of the region's commercial whalers were the Basques—a society of European seafarers and fishermen whose shore-based whaling stations may have already been operating in North America before the time of Columbus. By the middle of the sixteenth century, shore stations such as Buterus (Red Bay) on the Belle Isle Strait, together with others like it all around the seacoasts of northeastern Canada, were taking *two to three thousand whales per year* from this area.

Most of these stations were closed by the early decades of the seventeenth century due to the severe depletion of whale populations—but this was only the beginning of our species' collective assault on the great whales. Shore stations were replaced by small, fast whaling sloops, then by larger ships with greater range and stowage capacity, and finally by floating factories that could put to sea for years at a time while literally circling the Earth in search of their prey.

Five hundred years ago, according to Canadian naturalist Farley Mowat, the Gulf of St. Lawrence might better have been called the Gulf of Whales, so plentiful were these creatures here. This vast area of nearly landlocked sea was a natural haven where whales of almost every species could assemble to breed and multiply, and the waters abounded with their presence.

On a summer evening five centuries later, however, there was no longer such profusion. The fin whales my shipmates and I encountered that night were but a small remnant of what once had been a master race. Did these individuals represent the final fifth? The final tenth? The final hundredth of their kind? Whatever the percentage, these were the survivors of five centuries of slaughter visited by one species upon another. Yet they did not retaliate. Their genetic coding, it seemed, did not allow it—and they remained perhaps the only true pacifists nature has ever produced.

I'm not sure why so many in our present generation have turned to watching the great whales. Perhaps for some of the same reasons that my shipmates and I did so that night. The whales serve as a reminder to our kind both of who we are and what we have been doing to the Earth. As an order of living organisms hundreds of times larger and forty times more ancient than our own, they are an expression of the sheer exuberance of the evolutionary process. Their presence on this planet humbles us; their decimation shames us. They are a race of giants so serene and so perfectly adapted to their natural setting that they emerge as exemplary models (if only we will allow them) of peace and balance and decorum in nature.

That evening in the Gulf of St. Lawrence, my shipmates and I waited in silence as the last of the twilight disappeared from the western horizon. The wind dropped to a whisper, and the sailboat ghosted at a knot or two across glassy seas. Somewhere ahead a deep, guttural rush of air sounded in the darkness. Then another, closer by. And a third, dead ahead. Finally in the black of night the breathing of the whales came to seem like something more: a world breath, a *spiritus mundi* signaling from the depths of the abyss, a sound not unlike the breathing of the sea itself, rising and falling like a living membrane of the planet it surrounds.

Varuna

In the ancient Hindu pantheon there is a god whose name is Varuna, the wind. According to the *Rig Veda*, Varuna is many things. Varuna is the air that whispers in the grass, the sea breeze that cools the shore, the gale that rattles the shutters and groans in the branches of trees. Varuna is also your own breath—unconscious, continuous, invisible sustainer of life—and by analogy, Varuna is the breath of the universe, the life-force, the pulse and rhythm of Being.

I like the idea that the world is a living, breathing thing. I like the thought that the wind you hear high up in the rigging of your ship in the dark of a summer night might also be the breathing of some kind of cosmic life-force. I like the Vedic circlings: the notion that the wind, breathing through your own breath, is also the universal life-breath that streams back into the breathing that is within you and that you understand, simply, as the wind.

There is a much more scientific way of talking about such things, of course. In meteorological circles, one refers to wind fields, stationary fronts, squall lines, omega blocks. The meteorological wind flows around migratory highs and lows, falling out and away from the domes of highs, tumbling down and into the depressions of lows. The air swirling around these systems moves along imaginary lines of equal barometric pressure called isobars, while the systems themselves slam into one another in fronts, mix in areas of turbulence, stack up in ridges, accelerate in shear zones.

North of the equator the air slipping off the domes turns in a clockwise direction while the air falling into the depressions turns in a counterclockwise direction, under the influence of a centrifugal force called the Coriolis effect, caused by the spinning of the Earth. South of the equator the directions are reversed. In each hemisphere there are also stationary features, called geographic highs and lows, that define a series of permanent wind fields:

the polar easterlies; the subtropical westerlies; the horse latitudes; the trade winds.

Which of these two descriptions of the wind is true—the Vedic or the scientific? There are many who would argue that one must make a choice, embracing the scientific description and rejecting the animistic one (or vice versa). There are many who would say that the two are logically inconsistent: that the ancient description is mystical and metaphorical and has no analogue in experience, whereas the modern description is orderly, systematic, and empirically verifiable.

Such a reaction would seem to make sense, especially from the perspective of one who lives within what Theodore Roszak calls "the mindscape of science." Yet I would beg to differ. For I think that to insist on making a choice between the two descriptions is to misunderstand what each is about and to ignore the ways that each may interface with and enrich the other.

Science is a map, a truth system, in the same way that the *Rig Veda* is also a map, a truth system. Neither one claims to be isomorphic with the reality it attempts to represent. Nor does either one require us to believe, literally, in the language it employs. Perhaps there is no *literal* deity named Varuna out there broadcasting its cosmic breath through the ship's rigging. But there are no literal "isobars" out there either, no real "domes," no actual "fronts," no physical "ridges." There is just air, behaving in sometimes peaceful, sometimes violent ways, moving in vast and complex patterns that are almost as difficult to comprehend and predict today as they were five thousand years ago.

The best meteorologist I know, specialty forecaster Bob Rice, uses a markedly *un*scientific vocabulary whenever he talks about the dynamic patterns of wind. Highs "wander" eastward. Depressions "run into tough going." The north wind "tries" to strengthen. Fronts "run out of gas." Hurricanes "move like balloons." Ridges "mush along."

What Rice reveals with his shamelessly metaphorical language is precisely what makes him such a good weather forecaster: he reveals his understanding that the wind acts as a dynamic living thing, that it operates in a realm somewhere beyond his scientific categories, and that, inevitably, it behaves with a mind and will of its own.

Rice's forecast office in mid-state New Hampshire is filled with computer screens and fax terminals and dedicated telephone lines through which he receives meteorological data from dozens of sources. Like all good meteorologists, he studies the data with fanatical zeal in order to get a feel for the endless permutations of weather and wind that swirl across the face of the planet. But unlike most of his meteorological colleagues, he does not base his forecasts solely on the computer models in front of him. Instead, he observes the data with an intuitive eye and adds the Bob Rice touch. He follows his hunches about what the wind "wants," and he makes educated guesses about what it may be "trying to do" next.

I've never talked with Bob Rice about Varuna, but I suspect he would have no particular problem with someone who wanted to describe the wind as a sort of animistic persona—or even with the notion that this persona might be conceived as the breath and life-force of the planet. The energy that science describes as the meteorological wind is, after all, merely a manifestation of the Earth's quintessential source of energy: the sun. Even the most literal-minded scientist should have no trouble affirming this connection.

When it comes to thinking about the wind, I want to make use of both the scientific truth system and the Vedic truth system. The two methods of understanding speak to different faces of the same phenomenon, and together they define and circumscribe the thing in a way that neither can do by itself. This evening the wind is blowing from the north-northwest at force three to four, backing into the east over the next twelve hours as a deepening low approaches. This evening the wind is also Varuna, the universal life-force, the cosmic analogue to our own breathing. It is the voice that whispers in the rigging of our ship, speaking of change and mortality, telling us about the beauty of this night, warning of the storm to come.

Feeding the Sea Gods

There comes a moment early in every long offshore sailing passage when somebody on board suggests that maybe it's time to make an offering to the sea gods—just in case they're feeling a little cantankerous. The sea gods, somebody else explains, are unpredictable. You never know when they might decide to brew up a line squall or a rogue wave or a three-day nor'east gale. Sometimes they'll do it because you've forgotten to make the required offering (cookies, usually, tossed over the stern); other times they'll do it just for the pure hell of it.

Making an offering to the sea gods is always a quasi-comic affair. Somebody laughs. Somebody else grimaces and warns (with the ancient power of prophecy) that the sea gods always punish unbelievers. Then the cookies are passed around and an ad hoc priest offers the incantation: "to Varuna," or "to Ralph," or "to the Old Man of the Sea." The cookies are sacrificed to the wind, the crew raises a cheer, and everybody feels a little better, somehow.

What is it about this ritual sacrifice to the sea gods that always seems so necessary on the first day at sea? I've often wondered, after the ceremony is over, why we've all seemed to take it so seriously. Isn't this whole business really just an elaborate joke?

Yes and no. It *is* a joke, of course—a kind of comic hide-and-seek with the unsolved mysteries of existence. But it's also serious: a sailor's prayer, a gesture about how we are connected with the natural world.

Something odd happened once upon a time in the evolution of human consciousness when our forefathers first began to think about the idea of a monotheistic God. The ancient animistic religions had been religions of in-dwelling. The gods were many; they lived inside of things. Sometimes they actually *were* things. And then along came the idea of a singular, exclusive, indivisible God, and I guess because He couldn't be everywhere at once, He was conceived as being somehow above or beyond or outside the world of things. This God was abstracted into a being "wholly Other." He was conceived as residing in a dualistic universe of heaven and Earth, God and creation, "up there" and "down here."

Over the millennia this dualistic view of reality became the foot-in-the-door for science. Not right away. But in a few thousand years, after people had grown comfortable with the idea of God "out there," they finally were willing to reify all the rest of His creation "down here"— to envision it as spiritless, dead matter. One of the tenets of the scientific worldview, in fact, is just this: matter that has no spirit. Physical reality demystified. Trees without voices. Hills that don't weep. Thunder that doesn't know how to threaten. Wind that can't be angry.

In-dwelling spirit has been out of fashion (in the Western world, at least) for quite some time now. So much so that when you mention something like sea gods, people laugh. When you hang an amulet on the wall or set a coin under the mast, or touch a lucky stone in your pocket, people look oddly at you and wonder if you've gone a little funny in the head.

Yet part of what I'm looking for—and part of what a lot of other people seem to be looking for these days—is a deeper sense of the in-dwelling spirit in things. People go sailing on the ocean in small boats to feel connected. But how can you feel connected to dead matter? How can you figure out where you are or why you're here or what your living means when everything around you is lifeless, quantifiable, manipulable "stuff"? When the only mystery lies in what you haven't yet counted, weighed, measured, taken apart, and put back together again?

"God is in the details," writes the poet Brendan Galvin. Let's do the poet one better: maybe—just maybe—God *is* the details.

If you want to know where you are or why you're here or what your living means, look to the physical world. Listen to it. Touch it. Breathe it. If you want to know how the universe works, watch the seabirds, stare at the pattern of waves, study the clouds. Contemplate the intricacy and interconnectiveness of things. Climb out of your self. Get over the hang-up that you have been created in God's image. Stop postulating a deity who has turned His back on all the rest of creation and focused His attention on one rather pathetic bipedal species. Let the universe come alive again with gods of all shapes and sizes—let it be filled in every part with in-dwelling spirit.

The astonishing thing, on leaving the land and sailing off on a long ocean voyage, is how quickly most people seem willing to embrace the old superstitions. Offering cookies to Ralph; setting coins under the mast;

rubbing lucky stones; raising toasts to Varuna and the Old Man. One reason, I suspect, is the vulnerability we all feel at sea. We're far enough away from the routines of home to sense that the familiar magic may not be enough out here. Like the Norse voyagers who readily worshiped the gods of any place they happened to visit, we, too, become theologians of expediency. Who among us knows, really, which deity is the most powerful out here? Maybe we should just pay homage to as many as we can.

I've seen members of an offshore crew become anxious if we miss even one ritual feeding of the sea gods. I've watched half-sick shipmates bring the box of cookies up on deck in the middle of a stormy passage, hand them out, and lead the offertory themselves. Why? Maybe they're just performing a mariner's version of Pascal's Bet. (We win if there is a Varuna; we don't lose if there isn't one.) Or maybe they're doing something more . . . maybe they're making a ritual gesture of assent to the mysterious forces that in-dwell in the ocean wilderness.

In the end, the real joke is in the thought that the sea gods care whether we offer them cookies or not. Of course they don't care. The cookies are for us—not them. The cookies are the means by which we remind ourselves of our inconsequence. But they are also a way of affirming that we are part of whatever is going on out here. Not the prime mover. Maybe not even a very important participant. But part, at least: one small player in the cosmic dance.

I love what it means to feed cookies to the sea gods. It means that we've affirmed the spirit in things—and that we understand, in a funny way, that we are connected.

The following is excerpted from a letter written to a friend and former shipmate, Beth Hawkins, a crew member aboard Brendan's Isle *on a voyage to Labrador in 1988. Several years later, Beth was traveling around the United States in an old beat-up Volkswagen, trying to figure out what both she and America were all about. She had just written me a long and rambly letter—a kind of speculative foray from a person in mid-process. In it she posed a pair of questions that travelers typically ask—questions about where she was going and why in the world she was going there.*

The Breath of Being

Dear Beth,

Thanks for taking time to write. I enjoyed your remarks about "where" and "why." As I'm sure you know, the second question is always the hardest for a traveler— even as it is probably also the most important. Sometimes, though, the answer to this kind of question doesn't come in words. Sometimes it only comes in the actual doing of a thing—as part of the process of the journey.

Speaking of journeys, I've decided to sail *Brendan's*

Isle to Labrador again next summer. Why? I'm not exactly sure. All I know is that the idea feels right. Words and reasons and speculations notwithstanding, the "why" may finally have to emerge just as it did last time: among a group of travelers living and working together across four thousand miles of getting there and getting home again.

With all the highway miles you've been driving lately, I'm wondering if you still find the time to go jogging once in a while. I continue to be something of an addict in that regard. I was jogging this morning, in fact, letting my mind wander in a random sort of way, when I began thinking back to some of the wild-eyed speculations that you and I used to share during our watch times together aboard *Brendan's Isle.*

Do you remember the day we were talking about prayer—both the kind you learn to repeat as a child and the kind that just seems to happen by itself? Well, for some reason, I began thinking this morning about that conversation—then about the Lord's Prayer. Thinking, actually, about how uncomfortable I've always been with the language of that traditional prayer—with the double-layered geography of heaven and Earth and with the paternalistic and martial imagery of an almighty Father who seems so distant from the realm of this-world. Maybe it's the sailor in me—but I've always felt that the universe and whatever unnameable deity there is that resides here must be much more connected somehow.

Anyway, as I was jogging this morning, breathing in and breathing out (which has always seemed its own kind of prayer to me), I found myself mentally rewriting the words that we were taught to say in church and that we've repeated so many times. The result sounds a little like the poetry of the Vedic philosophers, a little like the theology of Paul Tillich, a little like the speculations of Alan Watts. I'm sure it is all of these things, with a large dose of the North Atlantic Ocean thrown in.

I hope you don't mind if I presume to try this one out on you. Not in any effort to persuade—but merely in the spirit of those cockpit theologies we used to share on sunny afternoons along the coast of Nova Scotia. Think of this as one of those prayers that happens by itself, whispered to the sounds of creaking sails and the surge of the bow wave and the hissing of the wake as it trails off the stern.

O Breath of Being
That moves in every molecule of creation,
And that is so boundless as to have no name,
Thy kingdom is now,
Thy will is manifest in all that is,
On Earth as in the farthest galaxies.

Give us this day the means to understand beyond our
     selves;
Give us the courage to affirm our own inconsequence;
Give us the wisdom to love the world and celebrate our
     oneness with it.

Teach us how to dance and how to laugh,
Help us to affirm the laughter of others,
And deliver us from desire.

For thou art all life and all matter, all motion and all
     time,
Beyond good and evil,
Beyond persuasion and prayer,
Impersonal and entire,
The breath of every now, through all the aeons of the
     universe.

Amen.

     In the ivy halls of the great universities, the sort of
theology that informs this prayer might be labeled "mon-
ism" (that is, "one-ism" or "single-ism"), as if by calling
something an "ism" you might then be able just to file it
away in a convenient cubbyhole and move on to the next
topic.
     But no matter. Cubbyhole or not, this sort of prayer

feels right to me—a little like the decision to sail to Labrador again. I'm not sure why it feels right—maybe the only answer is in the doing of it (or in this case the saying of it, the thinking about it, the actual *breathing* of it as you jog along).

Please write again when you get another moment in your travels. I won't ask for any speculations as to "why"—just "where" and how it's all been going.

Much love—

Mike

If You See the Buddha,
Kill Him

There's a line from one of Bob Dylan's early songs in which the singer describes himself as "born to too many choices." A curious thought—but when you stop to think about it, maybe also an accurate way of describing a lot of people today. Because increasingly in a world of instantaneous electronic communications we are able to ignore the traditional boundaries that have kept people and nations, cultures and ideas, philosophies and religions insulated from one another. We live in a huge informational melting pot in which we have access not just to one way of thinking or behaving but to the broad spectrum of human thought and endeavor.

It may still be possible in such a world to grow up as an Amish farmer or a Hasidic Jew or a Trappist monk. But the cost is high, requiring as it does a virtual withdrawal from the settings in which most people live. For the rest of us, the mindscape of our daily lives has become kaleidoscopic. The choices we face—about what to believe in, what values to hold, what directions to point our lives—are nearly endless.

Sometimes the choices feel overwhelming. I have known these times, as most of us have. Then it is tempting to wish for simpler lives, for systematized belief systems, and for unambiguous answers. But more often for me, the complexity of a world whose doors have been thrown open to the farthest reaches of human possibility feels like an invitation to search for what is true.

Living in a world of choices is dangerous, for it also means living in a world full of half-truths and dead ends, full of narcotic dreams and false prophets. It means setting out on a journey without a map or a ready set of guidelines passed down by our elders. When we are seeking to learn what is true—and I'm convinced that every person spends an important part of his life seeking to learn what is true—then we necessarily become spiritual and intellectual explorers. Like millions of others in the informational melting pot, I have become a spiritual and intellectual explorer.

One of the paths that I explored—many years ago when I was still a student at the university—led back in time more than twenty-six hundred years to a body of wisdom literature known as the Dhammapada. This is a collection of teachings and stories about a man whose followers called him Buddha—the Blessed One. Oddly enough, the tale of this man's life is in certain ways like the tale of millions of our own lives—for just as his modern counterparts, he was also a spiritual and intellectual explorer.

There is a set of texts in the Dhammapada that have had Buddhist scholars arguing about their meaning for centuries. Together they comprise a compelling and timeless story that establishes this enigmatic Indian wise man as unique among the great teachers of the world. The story goes like this:

One day when Buddha, the Blessed One, was nearing that state of spiritual perfection that his followers understood as Nirvanic bliss, he sat in his customary attitude of meditation under the Bhodi tree surrounded by a group of his disciples. Ananda, his most dedicated student, posed a question that had been troubling him for a long time.

"When you leave this world, O Master, when I am alone and wandering on an unfamiliar road, how shall I determine which direction to proceed? How shall I recognize the way of truth?''

The Blessed One sat for a moment in silence, as if he had not heard Ananda's question. Then he looked sternly at his disciple and admonished him: "If you see the Buddha on the road, kill him."

Ananda was visibly shaken by his master's words. "But, O Enlightened One, without your guidance, how shall I know which path to choose? How shall I be certain that I am following the way that you would have me go?"

Buddha softened his voice almost to a whisper. "When I am no longer with you, Ananda, you must work out your own salvation with diligence."

Small wonder that Buddhist scholars have been arguing about this story for two and a half millennia. Its implications are nothing short of revolutionary. Some traditionalists have suggested that what Buddha really meant was "if you see a false Buddha—an impersonator—kill him." But this is not what Buddha said. In the simplest and most direct language he could use, the Enlightened One instructed his follower to kill the teacher.

I would like to think that Buddha meant exactly what he said. But if this is so—then what did Buddha mean?

Elsewhere in the Dhammapada there are many dialogues about the truth that human beings seek. According to the ancient wisdom, truth (substitute "love," "peace," "Brahman," "God," "order," "ground") is an absolute.

It supersedes all the imperfect descriptions that we may construct for it. It does not depend on whether you or I "believe" in it. It is like one of Plato's ideal forms—that is to say, it exists beyond the specific opinions that we, individually or collectively, might have about it.

If this is so, if the shape and organization and ground of our being is indeed ultimate and absolute, if it simply "is" and does not depend on our particular conceptualizations of it, then, assuming the seeker is diligent in his quest, whatever way he chooses to search will lead him to his goal. For as the ancient saying goes, "He who travels to the left will meet he who travels to the right" and all roads will eventually lead to the omega point.

For those of us who, like Ananda, are looking for a set of instructions, a road map that will point the way, this thought can be pretty frightening. Because what it suggests is that each of us is radically free: free to search in the best way we know how. What it means is that the Trappist monk is on the right road. But so is the Hasidic Jew. And so is the Amish farmer. And so are you, and so am I. Just as long as each of us is honest and diligent in our quest, then we are going together toward the same omega point.

If there is one important insight that our cultural and informational melting pot would seem to teach us, it is that knowledge, especially knowledge about the truth, is not a commodity. It is not a "thing" to be passed on as some sort of prepackaged formula. Because there are too many ways, too many systems, too many choices. There are too many seekers, each following a different path. There is no convenient perspective from which we can compare and pass judgment, calling one way right and all the others wrong.

When the Buddha tells Ananda to kill him, what exactly is he saying? One thing that he is not saying is something another great teacher once voiced to his disciples: "I am the Light and the Truth and the Way. Follow me and ye shall find the Kingdom of Heaven." Rather, he is saying that you cannot learn the truth by means of imitation—not by following a prescribed formula—not by merely obeying a set of rules. Buddha himself was a rebel and an iconoclast. Much of the story of his life is the story of his rejection of the stale wisdom of the Hindu tradition in which he grew up. Buddha himself was an explorer, a seeker in a wilderness of choices. And Buddha followed no Buddha.

In a perverse sort of way, the Buddha seems to be telling Ananda to act just as Buddha did. "Do not follow me in some mindless, imitative fashion," he is saying. "Kill me. And work out your own salvation with diligence."

And what do such words mean for someone living at the dawn of the twenty-first century? To me, they mean several things:

—We are all seekers.

—None of us has a monopoly on the truth.

—There are many paths. Don't be too quick or harsh to judge. What may work for you may not work for me—and vice versa.

—The path one follows may be by reason of culture or heritage or temperament. Each can work if the search is honest, unselfish, diligent.

—In the end (and what is that?) the paths will intersect. Because in the end the objective is something that *is*, independent of what any of us may claim to know.

. . . in the East they still preserve the once universal concept: that wandering reestablishes the original harmony which once existed between man and the universe.

—Bruce Chatwin, *The Songlines*

Wandering

Brendan's Isle strains at her anchor in a deserted cove in northern Newfoundland. I lie in my bunk with a book propped in front of me, listening to the rain driving against the decks and cabin tops and the wind groaning in the rigging. The ship's clock strikes six o'clock—and I gaze out through a porthole at the gray light of dawn and the black mottled boulders at the edge of the cove.

None of my shipmates is awake yet, and I realize that there is still another hour before the routines of the vessel are due to begin. I close the book I've been reading and stare at the overhead, and I start thinking about something that people living ashore might not be able to understand. I start thinking about how right it feels to be here, traveling in a little sailboat on a nearly deserted coast, forty-five days and two thousand miles from home.

Am I simply describing what it feels like to be living an obsession? Yes—this is part of it. Traveling under sail to the remote coasts of the northern Atlantic basin has become the one thing I'd choose to do no matter how cold the rain or how strong the wind or how many miles from home the journey happened to lead. Yet this morning I find myself wondering if there might also be something more—something rooted in the ancient past and imprinted in the genetic memory of our species—something that wants a journey like this and that makes it feel like the most natural enterprise that a human being could undertake.

There has been a good deal of speculation in scientific circles lately about what life must have been like for our evolutionary predecessor, *Homo habilis*, back in the Rift Valley of eastern Africa two and a half million years ago. Clearly, this is a subject that no one will ever be able to probe with a great deal of accuracy. But there is a growing fossil record that has provided some clues, and there are climatological indicators that now suggest that this new species was evolved during the onset of the modern period of glaciation in the northern hemisphere—an ice age that transformed the African rain forest into a semiarid region of open woodlands, extensive grasslands and undependable water sources.

Part of the story of *Homo habilis* can be pieced together from his fossil remains. Numerous indicators, from the tilt of his pelvis and the raised arch in his feet to the rapid increase in the size of his cranium, indicate that this creature had now become a two-limb walker and a forager of the open savannah rather than a sedentary, four-limb forest ape like his predecessor, *Australopithecus africanus*. The new proto-man was thus in all likelihood a migratory species. Through the process of natural selection, he had developed a way to pursue the continual search for food and water required by the desert-like conditions in which he found himself. Wandering became his genetic preference, his knee-jerk response to the world, as well as his most dependable strategy for survival.

In our own century the psychological importance of the ancient memories that we carry around in our genes was first recognized by the great neo-Freudian psychoanalyst Carl Jung, primarily in the context of dream analysis and the symbolism of what he called the "collective unconscious." More recently, an entire school of so-called "evolutionary psychology" has emerged, centering around the idea that modern man, *Homo sapiens sapiens*, is an evolutionary species like all others—a creature whose instincts, fears, desires, needs, social patterns, linguistic and intellectual aptitudes are all strongly influenced by genetic codings imprinted in his DNA during his ancient past.

Man, the citizen of urban industrial society, has only been living on the planet for a few hundred years. Man, the agriculturalist and village-dweller, has been here for a mere ten thousand years more. Neither time span is nearly long enough on an evolutionary time scale for *Homo sapiens sapiens* to have adapted through natural selection to the sedentary lifestyle that both forms of social organization have enforced upon him and that most human beings now lead. Thus, even though we are typically rooted to a village or town or city and think of ourselves as "urbanized," it is likely that our DNA still posits us as wanderers and that somewhere deep within our psychic beings we remember the ancient pathways.

One of the most provocative investigations to have appeared in recent years about humankind's genetic memory as a migratory species is to be found in Bruce Chatwin's *The Songlines*, his now-classic exploration of the "dreaming tracks" of the Australian aborigines. Chatwin, a traveler himself for most of his life, journeys to one of the last places on the Earth inhabited by tribes of hunter-gatherers—the Australian desert—and here he searches for the roots of his own longings to wander across the face of the world.

Wandering

Why, Chatwin asks, is humankind the most restless and dissatisfied of species? Why do wandering peoples conceive the world as perfect whereas sedentary ones seem always set on changing it? Why do townsfolk draw boundary lines, build walls, fight bloody territorial wars, whereas migratory groups seldom even entertain the notion of private property? Where does the ancient custom arise that walking dissolves crimes of violence? Why do the great prophets and teachers, from Christ to the Buddha, always gesture toward the road as the way to salvation?

Chatwin fashions answers to these questions for himself and his readers. But any wanderer can do the same, looking to the world to frame the questions, then consulting his own experience for answers.

Ask any traveler why he takes to the road—and why he seems so satisfied and filled with simple joy whenever he is on the move. Most of the answers you hear will begin to sound oddly similar, whether you find yourself talking to a walker or a touring cyclist or a climber or a canoeist or an ocean sailor.

"The journey just feels right," the traveler will tell you. "The focus on the goal gives my living a kind of direction and meaning. The routines of the day: preparing meals, packing, breaking camp, moving to the next destination, setting up camp again . . . have an oughtness to them. The routines provide a feeling of permanence. Yet the journey is a movable feast. I'm never bored. Each destination is fresh and new. When I'm traveling I never seem to worry about tomorrow—or yesterday. All time on the journey feels like present time. And I'm never lonely. There is a camaraderie among travelers. I always feel that I'm among helpers and friends."

It is impossible to tell for sure whether such responses are evidence of a deep psychic need for the structures and disciplines of a journey—or whether they are merely a reaction that any healthy human being would make to the tedium of a sedentary existence. Would we be better off as a species, as Chatwin sometimes insinuates, if we could leave the cities behind and follow the tracks of our ancestors? Would we stop the wars and the killing if we could somehow eliminate the boundaries we've drawn among our villages and cities and nations and return to the nomadic circlings of our earliest beginnings? Indeed, is the story we've been telling ourselves about our "progress" as a species during the last ten thousand years really upside-down? Have we actually *regressed*, psychologically, from a state of harmony with our natural surroundings to a state of boredom, contentiousness, and alienation?

These are some of the questions that revolve in my head this morning as I listen to the rain and stare at the overhead, waiting for my shipmates to awaken. Soon it will be time for me to light the galley stove and brew a pot of coffee, then to move to the navigation table and begin to pore over the charts and sailing directions for the upcoming day's passage. Meanwhile, the others will clean the cabins, scrub the decks, remove the sail covers, hoist and clean and stow the anchors. Then it will be time to begin this movable feast once more, to let go of yesterday and stop thinking about tomorrow, to focus on today and embrace the journey as if it were all of life.

In the summer of 1994, I and a group of shipmates sailed Brendan's Isle *to western Greenland to investigate the polar ice and to dramatize an emerging story about changing global climate. One entry in the ship's log recounts an episode a hundred miles north of the Arctic Circle in which my shipmate Pete Johanssen and I venture ashore to witness a wilderness setting the likes of which neither of us has ever seen. The upshot is an epiphany in which the land communicates its message and we attempt to comprehend.*

Ukivik Island

The sun at midnight lights the sky with a fiery orange glow. The shadows in the mountains underneath are purple and ultramarine. The visibility is nearly unlimited and the textures of the land are undistorted, as if there were no atmosphere in this place to filter the light.

Twenty kilometers to the east the flanks of Mount Isortup appear so close that you could reach out and touch them. Fifteen kilometers to the south, a series of peaks on the Natarnivinqup range remain in direct sunlight and burn with the same orange glow. At their base, three thousand meters below, the surface of Nordre Isortoq Fiord mirrors the color so that it, too, seems to be ablaze in the reflected light.

Pete and I stand at the crest of a meadow on Ukivik Island trying to comprehend this landscape. We have come ashore after dinner to wander among the remains of an abandoned village and to investigate a series of grassy mounds that are scattered about the meadow. These mounds turn out to be the collapsed roofs of traditional Inuit sod houses—the only visible remains of a village that had once been the administrative center and the most important settlement of this region.

We stand facing east, looking toward the mountains. Behind us is the island. Directly in front is the small protected harbor where *Brendan's Isle* lies at anchor. The harbor is flanked by a series of rock ledges. Beyond these are the mouths of several large fiords, including the massive Nordre Isortoq Fiord, one of the longest in western Greenland.

In spite of the tiny form of the anchored sailboat before us (or maybe because of it), this place has a strange, unsettling quality to it—as if we simply do not belong here. The physical size of the land is overwhelming. The signs of human passing are faint and quickly covered. There is no enduring human imprint—maybe that's it—or at least none that would indicate that our kind is in any way important to this place. The land exists in a time scale and answers to a purpose that is entirely independent of us—neither benevolent nor malevolent, neither kind nor unkind, but simply indifferent.

Pete and I stand in silence—unable, at least for the moment, to articulate all the feelings that this place evokes. I find myself thinking about time—about the tremendous geologic age of the objects we are looking at. The written record of our species' collective memory, what we call our "history," spans a period of something like ten thousand years. The ice trapped in the glacial bowl behind these mountains spans a period of twenty-five times our history (two hundred fifty thousand years). And the mountains—these span a period of ten thousand times the age of the ice (two and a half billion years) and more. Some of these mountains, in fact, are among the oldest physical objects on the planet.

For some reason, the idea of geologic time seems to have been resisted by even the most observant of our forebears until very recent times. Why? Maybe because of our distinctly human need to feel that we are at the center of things—that we are cosmically important. This, in combination with our ancient myths of creation, has kept us from noticing the obvious. Yet the truth of geologic time is written everywhere in the Earth—we have simply chosen for thousands of years to ignore the handwriting.

I have a strong feeling as I stand gazing out at these

mountains—one that has been growing for the last couple of weeks as we have traveled along this coast and that comes with particular clarity whenever we are confronted by a landscape like this. I feel small and insignificant—not unlike the way a sailor feels when he's been traveling for many days on the ocean. Only here the feeling is magnified by the experience not only of limitless space in two horizontal dimensions but also of the massive, superhuman scale of objects in all three dimensions.

Human beings who live their lives in such a landscape must have a different mental image of themselves, I think, than those from gentler, flatter, warmer places. Here the Earth is clearly master. Here there is no illusion of being in control. No amount of self-flattery can mask the fact that under the shadow of these mountains, we are the ones who are visitors—perhaps only temporary visitors at that.

I gaze across the meadow at Pete, then out at the sailboat, framed against the crimson light. Both seem so frail out here tonight—so laughably small. A gust of wind swirls up from the harbor, rattling the grass at my feet. I turn toward the beach where we've left the rubber dinghy, calling for Pete, and I shudder with the sudden cold.

In Wildness is the preservation of the World.
　—HENRY DAVID THOREAU, *Walking*

Landscape and Humanscape

The view from the window of US Air Flight 417 is breath-taking. Today is one of those perfect days for flying: a cloudless sky with the air so clear that you can see the median strip on the interstate and count the cows grazing in the fields from four miles up. Thirty minutes into the flight the forested ridges of western Pennsylvania give way to the flat checkerboard of farms and villages of northeast Ohio. On the horizon to the right is Lake Erie, and ahead, just on the nose of the airplane, is an area of blue haze that will soon become the skyline of Cleveland.

I'm traveling today from Philadelphia, Pennsylvania, to my mother's family farm in upstate Michigan, a trip I've made many times. The flight and the scenery are familiar, and on any other day I probably would be sleeping through both. But this day is different. Because on this day as I look out through the airplane window, I find myself staring at a scene that has suddenly been transformed in my mind from a benign and rather ordinary swath of midwestern American landscape to something much more disturbing: thousands upon thousands of square miles of humanscape.

As the aircraft passes over Ohio and crosses into southern Michigan, I stare at the checkerboard below, searching for even one small patch of ground that has not been altered in some way by the presence of human beings. Surely in all this vast territory there must be an acre or two that some member of my species has not lumbered or plowed or mined or built a road or house or factory on.

The more I look, however, the more I sense the futility of my looking. The forests and woodlots that still remain in Pennsylvania and Ohio and Indiana and Michigan are all third or fourth growth. The soils underneath the farms are renitrogenized production sites for feed corn and soybeans. The creeks and streams and lakes are bridged, dammed, diverted, fished, filled with effluents from surrounding farms and communities. Even Lake Erie, stretching along the horizon to the north and east like a huge inland sea, has long since been depleted of fish, poisoned by industrial and agricultural runoff, and capped by a layer of algae that has forever changed the structure of its ecosystem.

I suddenly realize that there is no natural landscape down there any longer. All of it, every square inch of it, has been transformed into something else by the millions of human beings who now live there.

I know that if I had been making this same trip a few years earlier, I probably would not have noticed anything unusual in the scene below. Mid-America has looked just about the same as it does today for as long as I can remember. The checkerboard geometries are actually rather pretty from several miles up. The spiderweb of roads makes fascinating patterns across the land. The cities look like scale models of something out of *Star Wars*.

Then something happened to me—an odd turn of events that started a few years ago and that has changed everything. For almost a decade I'd been operating a sail-training program for high school students along the northeastern seaboard of the United States. Then, with a new and stronger boat, I began recruiting groups of older sailors and taking them on summer voyages to places that most human beings never visit and in which almost no human beings live: first to the subarctic coasts of Labrador, then to the Arctic coasts of western Greenland. I've just returned from a voyage to Greenland, in fact, a few days before this flight, and my mind is still filled with images of jagged black mountains, steep fiords, huge rivers of moving ice—a blasted and empty landscape capped with the loom of the great central ice sheet and stretching for hundreds of miles with virtually no human imprint.

It is the contrast between the massive and impersonal landscapes of Greenland and the humanscapes of mid-America that has suddenly transformed the vista outside the airplane window and made it seem so disturbing to me. I've just had an encounter that many people living on the Earth today will never be able to experience—an encounter with raw nature—and it has altered the way I think about myself and my species and the way I look at this planet.

The fact is, in the latitudes where the majority of the Earth's human population now lives, there are fewer and fewer places that have not been transformed in some way by human activity. In most urban settings there is virtually nothing that remains of unaltered nature. More than 70 percent of us now live and work in such settings, and we have learned to adapt, by increments, to the humanscapes around us until we can hardly remember what a natural landscape looks like any longer.

This is a dangerous situation—because as we adapt to our own transformations of the natural world, we continually adjust our definition of what "nature" is. We drive through a region of cornfields and orchards and feedlots and imagine that we are in the "country." We park our RV's for the weekend in paved campsites with public toilets, running water, wheelchair ramps, cable TV hookups—and we start to think that this is what is meant by "wilderness." We swim in a quagmire of chemicals and floating trash and mistake this for the "ocean."

Most dangerous of all, we convince ourselves, perhaps because of the pervasiveness of the humanscape, that we are at the center of things—that we are the controllers, the "managers" of the planet. Surrounded on every side by the work of our own hands, many of us cannot even imagine a setting any longer that hasn't been lumbered, mined, plowed, planted, lined with buildings, connected with highways, bridged, mowed, fertilized, trimmed, paved, electrified, airportized, strung together with telephone wires, linked with TV dishes, computerized with E-mail, connected by the Internet.

An encounter with a natural landscape—of the sort that I and a group of young sailors were fortunate enough to experience this past summer—is vitally important, for it is a means of breaking the spell that we have cast upon ourselves. It may no longer be possible for all of us to contact the Earth directly—for we are now nearly six billion and there may literally not be enough of unaltered nature left to go around. But there are still plenty of ways to accomplish such an encounter—and those who have the opportunity must somehow devise ways to share their experiences with those who do not. For without such points of contact, we lose perspective on what is happening to us and to the Earth. We fall victim to our own misconceptions about the way nature works, forgetting that we are not the architects but only tenants of this place, cohabiting a planet that needs to include all.

Can [the entire biosphere] really be the outcome of nothing but a cascade of algorithmic processes feeding on chance? And if so, who designed that cascade? Nobody. It is itself the product of a blind, algorithmic process.
—DANIEL C. DENNETT, *Darwin's Dangerous Idea*

Darwin

There's been quite a stew in Western society for the last century and a half about an idea that a young Englishman brought home after a long sailing voyage and eventually had the impertinence to publish. The young man's name was Charles Darwin and the voyage, aboard an English hydrographic survey ship called the HMS *Beagle,* lasted nearly three years.

Many accounts have been written about the genesis of Darwin's idea, about the mountains of data that he collected, the huge packing crates of natural specimens that he shipped back to the British Museum, the influences of scientific contemporaries like Sedgwick and Henslow and of predecessors like Malthus and Hume. Relatively little attention has been paid, however, to the *setting* in which Darwin collected and organized his specimens and wrote all his preliminary notes and observations—the cabin of a full-rigged sailing ship en route across forty thousand miles of open ocean on its way on a three-year meander around the world.

Would Darwin have been able to speculate about the natural world in the revolutionary way that he did if he'd spent those three years at a desk in his father's home in Shrewsbury or in a study carrel at Christ Church College in Cambridge or in an office cubicle at the British Museum? I don't mean to ask whether he would have been able to collect the specimens—that activity required the voyage—but, rather, whether he would have been moved to perceive the algorithmic patterns of generation and relationship that eventually formed the basis of his world-transforming hypothesis?

My hunch is that all those weeks and months and years at sea had a lot to do with the formation of Darwin's idea. The experience that connected the Azores and Patagonia and the Galápagos Islands and New Zealand and Marturius and the Cape of Good Hope and all the species of crawling, flying, swimming things that inhabited those places was an experience of the deep ocean—a rhythmic, impersonal, oddly humbling experience of traveling across vast geographical distances and through a time continuum defined not by clocks or personal deadlines or national anniversaries but by the circlings of astronomical bodies and the ponderous turnings of the seasons.

The altogether startling thing about Darwin's theory of evolution is the randomness (some would say the mindlessness) of the process that underlies it: a process Darwin termed "natural selection." Darwin didn't know exactly how natural selection worked in particular organisms, for he lacked the idea of a gene or a string of DNA. But he recognized, in an intuitive way, that somehow it *did* work—that mutations occurred in all species as a matter of chance, and that a simple algorithmic formula when applied to such mutation would result in increasingly successful variations that would eventually predominate in what he termed "the struggle for existence."

The resulting scheme for the functioning of the natural world has turned Western science, philosophy, and religion all on their ears. The traditional "top-down" worldview in which God, the Perfect Mind, creates all lesser beings has become, with Darwin, a "bottom-up" worldview in which mindless pattern takes on the creative role and chance becomes the generative force. In Darwin's scheme of things, the tree of life grows as a fractal structure, nonlinear, open-ended, generating out of chaos, moving toward greater and greater complexity. Curiously, it grows according to some of the same principles of randomness and nonlinearity as the wind, the pattern of waves, the generation of clouds, the progression of storms across the face of the deep. Is it just coincidence that the genesis of Darwin's theory of evolution began on a sailing ship at sea? Or did the ocean setting somehow precondition his thinking and provide a kind of shadowy paradigm?

It's going to be up to the philosophers and theologians to try to cope with the havoc that Darwin's theory has left in its wake. Meanwhile, however, Western science has unanimously embraced the idea, researchers have turned to investigating mechanisms, and everyday citizens have been provided a new way of thinking about themselves and their place in nature.

There have been misunderstandings, of course. The most persistent of these came at the hands of a group of economists and social scientists at the turn of the last century. This group called themselves "social Darwinists" and popularized the phrase "the survival of the fittest." The phrase has long since been debunked, both as a slogan of social philosophy and as an explanation of Darwin's theory—although for a number of reasons it has stuck around as a handy cliché in the popular imagination.

The most articulate rebuttal of the notion of the survival of the fittest that I've read comes from Lewis Thomas, a medical doctor and self-appointed "biology watcher," who writes with passion and learning about the high incidence of cooperative behavior to be found everywhere in nature. He enumerates symbiotic relationships, from the pairings of crabs and anemones to the colonization of our own cells by centrioles, basil bodies, and hordes of mitochondria "without [which] we would not move a muscle, drum a finger, think a thought." All living organisms in Darwin's scheme vie for a place where they can succeed in the struggle for existence. Yet the way to success, surprisingly often, is not to compete but to form cooperative alliances with other organisms larger or smarter or older or uglier or stronger or quieter or more patient, and then just strike a low profile and tag along.

Another common misunderstanding of Darwin's theory relates to this notion of "success," especially as regards the human species. It is commonly assumed that since we are one of the brainiest and most influential organisms on the planet, we must also be one of the most successful. I made the mistake of stating such an assumption once in a conversation with a friend—a friend who happened to be a fossil biologist and the chairman of the Department of Earth and Planetary Sciences at Johns Hopkins University.

My friend rolled his eyes. "In my business we don't

consider a species 'successful' until it has a fossil record of twenty million years or so. *Homo sapiens* hasn't even been around for a million yet." With this he turned, pulled open the drawer of a specimen cabinet behind him, and handed me a pair of clam shells. "Now *here*'s an example of a successful species. The one in your right hand is a modern clam . . . the one in your left is a fossil from a road cut . . . about forty million years old. If I mix them up and give them back to you, I defy you to tell the difference."

The measure of a species' success, according to Darwin's scheme, has to do with numbers. All species tread a thin line. They can either fail to reproduce enough offspring—in which case they eventually become extinct—or they can reproduce too many, increase their population exponentially, and outgrow (surprisingly quickly) the capacity of their natural setting to support them. Clams, my friend explained, have found a niche where they seem able to get along with their neighbors, find adequate nutrition, and reproduce just enough new clams to replicate themselves. As long as the niche is there, the clams probably will be, too.

One final misinterpretation of Darwin's theory has to do with the question of where evolution ends. In the top-down worldview that many of us still share, we've gotten used to the idea that there *is* an end to evolution . . . and that we're it. We are the organism with the rational mind, and according to the ancient wisdom, there can be no higher form in nature.

In the bottom-up worldview of Darwinian evolution, however, there is no such endpoint. The generation of new forms is ongoing, and our species, like any other, is merely an evolutionary stepping-stone on the way to somewhere else.

This idea is admittedly a little scary. It is also somewhat deflating to a creature who has assumed for millennia that he sits on top of the heap. Yet, if you think about it for a moment, maybe this idea isn't nearly as scary as the other, rather apocalyptic notion that we are the final act. I mean if we really *are* the final act, then what comes next? A biblical conflagration? A Mars-like wasteland of empty rivers and red dust? A nuclear winter?

No . . . on weighing the alternatives, I think I'll go along with my biologist friend at Johns Hopkins. If for some miraculous reason we survive as a species for another nineteen million years, then we, too, will be able to join the ranks of the clams and count ourselves successful. If we don't make it that long, I hope we have the common decency, at least, to step aside, leave the rest of nature alone, and allow the process of natural selection to carry on without us.

The earth risks being eutrophied by us. We are now the dominant feature of our own environment.
    —LEWIS THOMAS, *The Lives of a Cell*

A Lesson in Simple Geometry

During a train ride to New York a few years ago I ran into an old friend—let's call him Alan—whom I hadn't seen in nearly a decade. Both of us had some time to kill, and we spent the rest of the journey catching up on what we'd been doing with our lives, then talking about some of the issues and ideas that were presently concerning us. Before the trip was over I found myself describing a research project I was then pursuing on the subject of changing global climate and the warning signals that seem to be emerging from the Arctic ice.

Alan listened attentively, interjecting a comment from time to time. Yet as we talked, I noticed a frown forming around the edges of his mouth. I'd been commenting on the accelerating use of fossil fuels at almost every level of human society, the increasing concentrations of carbon dioxide in the Earth's atmosphere, and the seemingly inevitable connection between these and changing patterns of global climate. The more I talked, however, the more I realized that Alan was not at all comfortable with the correspondences I was proposing. And eventually I came to understand why.

Alan is a gentle, thoughtful human being. He is a person, like many others, who has a deep and abiding faith in the ability of our planet to adjust to the changing stresses that it encounters (and that it *has* encountered for four and a half billion years). He is a man with a healthy ego, who cannot imagine himself—or his species—ever being powerful enough to change the Earth. He is an avid reader, a thinker, a student of geology, who can talk knowledgeably about giant meteor strikes in the ancient past that may have caused mass extinctions—or about huge volcanic eruptions that filled the atmosphere with aerosols of ash and dust and that may have led to sudden, catastrophic alterations in global climate. But he cannot even conceive a situation in which the collective actions of human beings might exercise the same kind of power to alter the planet we live on.

I wish I could still think the way Alan thinks. I wish I could still believe in the infinite self-healing power of the Earth and perceive the actions of humankind as small and insignificant. But I know Alan is wrong—and I know why. Alan has not taken a careful look at what is happening to the size of the human population of the Earth. And he does not understand the power of the exponent.

It is probably true that ten million human beings could not seriously impact this planet or alter its future course. But can the same be said of a hundred million human beings? A thousand million? Ten thousand million? The question, as we continue to multiply our numbers, is not whether human beings can change the Earth but only what magnitude of human activity is required to effect the change.

The history of human population growth since the beginning of the modern era presents a sobering picture. At A.D. 1 the total global population was somewhere in the neighborhood of two hundred fifty million people. The first doubling of this number required more than a millennium and a half, with global population reaching five hundred million by about 1600. The next doubling, to one billion, required only two hundred thirty years, culminating in about 1830. And the next doubling, to two billion, required a mere one hundred years, culminating in about 1930.

After 1930 the curve on the graph of human population growth begins to soar nearly straight up, with a third billion added to the total by 1960, a fourth billion by 1974, a fifth billion by 1986, and a sixth billion by the end of 1999. The doubling time has now dropped to under forty years, which means that every person living on Earth who is forty or older has now witnessed a doubling of global population—the first time such an event has occurred in the history of the human species.

It is commonly assumed that the story of human population growth over the past two thousand years can be described mathematically by means of an exponential progression. The truth, however, is even more alarming. For most of this period, until about 1700, the historical curve is actually much flatter than the exponential curve. Then, as doubling times decrease, the historical curve begins to steepen. By about 1850 it plots approximately parallel to the exponential curve. Then, after about 1930, it grows nearly vertical—steeper than the exponential curve—nearly as steep as Heinz Von Foerster's so-called "doomsday curve," a hypothetical projection that tracks the growth of the human population of the Earth to infinity by 2026.

No one in the scientific world is yet able to forecast with accuracy exactly how the rate of population growth may change in the coming decades, for there are too many variables that come into play as we approach the limits that the Earth itself will impose (already is imposing) upon the process. But as we approach these limits, there are a number of changes that *can* be predicted, all of them having to do with the impact of human activity upon natural systems. Our ever-expanding requirements for the production of food will continue to threaten natural habitats on a global scale and will lead to an accelerating rate of species extinctions. Our waste stream will continue to enter the atmosphere, the lakes and rivers, the oceans, the forests, and will alter the chemistry of all these places.

The buildup of CO_2 and other greenhouse gasses in the atmosphere and the likelihood of human-induced climate change are only two of the forecast outcomes. Others include the severe stressing or collapse of the world fishery, the desertification of large areas of formerly arable land, the depletion of subterranean water tables, the drying up of rivers, the large-scale poisoning of forests by acid rain. The "doomsday scenario" will not have to wait until the population soars to infinity. It will occur in increments (and is) as the human population draws ever closer to the limits that the Earth imposes upon it.

"The simple truth," writes Canadian environmentalist David Suzuki, "is that we are the last generation on Earth that can save this planet." Whether we are actually the last—or only close to the last—is perhaps a moot point. Our location on the graph of population growth argues that our time is running out. The direction of the growth curve is nearly vertical. Doubling time has collapsed into a matter of decades, and the magnitude of the doubling continues to grow. (The present doubling adds three billion people to the population of the planet; the next doubling will add *six* billion.)

Now, at the end of the 1990s, our numbers are growing at the rate of another Tokyo every three months, another Germany every year, the entire population of the planet in 1830 every thirteen years. The implications of this meteoric rise are mind-boggling. We're running out of time to reproduce infrastructure (houses, roads, schools, hospitals, means of food production, systems of distribution)—and even if we had enough time, we're running out of resources and physical space. The resultant dilemma is almost impossible for most of us to grasp. No wonder Alan didn't understand (or didn't want to understand) what was happening. Yet in the end he *must be made to understand*—because in the end it will be Alan, along with all the rest of us, who will be called upon to act.

We, the six billion, are no longer just another species cohabiting the planet but are now the single most powerful influence on Earth affecting global systems. This is what Lewis Thomas means when he describes us as "the dominant feature of our own environment." It is as if we have been waging a war and now, having nearly won, we've finally come to realize that the enemy we've been fighting has been the natural realm that has nurtured and sustained us during all the centuries of battle. Just as we've achieved dominance over virtually every other living thing, we've learned that if we want to survive this war, we will need to reverse our tactics and figure out a way to replenish the realm we set out to conquer.

Together, we have the ability to dramatically reduce our rate of population growth *within a single generation.* Meanwhile, we can also change our patterns of consumption, reduce our use of fossil fuels and other chemical substances, curtail our wholesale destruction of nonhuman habitats. All these and more are at least theoretically possible—if enough of us become conscious of the problem *soon* enough—and if we realize that we are the only ones left who have even the slightest hope of devising a solution.

Water Colors

After a long summer voyage to Canada, the final offshore passage for *Brendan's Isle* always begins in southern New England. From here she travels three hundred miles across the New York Bight, then ascends the Delaware River estuary another sixty miles to the Chesapeake and Delaware Canal and the headwaters of the Chesapeake Bay.

This year *Brendan's* track across the New York Bight has been dictated by southwesterly headwinds that have forced her farther and farther out to sea. On the morning when she's finally able to tack toward shore again, she is located two days south of New England, well beyond the continental shelf, in an area of the ocean where the water is more than two miles deep.

Flipping over onto the port tack, my shipmate John and I find ourselves sailing only a few miles east of the Gulf Stream in a wilderness as empty and untamed as any in this part of the world-ocean. Yet a hundred thirty miles to the west are the Delaware capes and the entrance to the Delaware Bay—about twenty hours' sailing time at the rate we are traveling. With luck and good wind, we know that by some time tomorrow afternoon we'll be entering the C and D Canal and that five hours later we'll be home, moored in front of my farm on the northern Chesapeake Bay.

Many transformations take place on such a passage as you travel from the deep ocean into one of the most densely populated and highly industrialized coastal areas on the planet. Perhaps the most remarkable, however, is the transformation that happens to the color of the water.

In the abyss near the Gulf Stream, the ocean surface is indigo, a color so rich and dark that it seems to swallow the light. If the wind is blowing hard, as it is this day, the seas mount in inky phalanxes, topped with platinum crests and crisscrossed with lines of white spindrift. As in all warm oceans of the world, however, the clarity of this water belies a little-known fact: that warm, stable surface water supports only small quantities of microscopic organisms, and that without such essential nutrients at the base of the food chain, the tropical and subtropical oceans are actually deserts where few larger organisms are able to survive. The sunlight here tunnels into the troughs of seas seeking the shells of diatoms and the exoskeletons of copopods to reflect it back again, and, finding none, disappears into the blackness below.

Fifty miles to the west, the bottom of the sea rises in a steep precipice as *Brendan* sails up onto the North American continental shelf. Here, cold bottom water upwells from the abyss, mixing with surface layers, and the water color changes in increments from indigo to aquamarine to forest green. As we sail across the five-hundred-fathom contour, John spots a family group of pilot whales hunting for squid along the continental rise. At a hundred fathoms we see a school of bluefin tuna churning the surface, while gulls and terns wheel and dive above them. On the horizon we can just make out the superstructure of a commercial fishing boat—the first of many—and the funnel of a cargo ship heading north toward New York City.

Except for a slow increase in coastal traffic, there is little sign of human presence here. We sail past several discontinued dump sites that are invisible from the surface but still marked on the chart: a large, generalized waste site just seaward of the shelf break that had been used by the City of New York until 1992 for the disposal of municipal sewage sludge; and forty miles farther west, an area used by the city of Philadelphia, also for sewage sludge, and another operated by the DuPont Corporation until the early 1980s for the disposal of acid waste.

Sunset sees a freshening of the southwest breeze, and *Brendan* charges into the night, moving toward the Delaware coast at a steady seven knots. By sunrise next morning she is fifty miles closer to her destination and only a few miles from the buoy that marks the seaward end of the commercial traffic separation zone. As the light rises behind us, we still see only a handful of fishing boats on the horizon—no ships, no legions of pleasure craft, no silhouettes of buildings on the shore. But even without such indicators, we realize that the coast is near, for we have now entered an area of tidal mixing where seawater and bay water collide, and once again the surface color changes dramatically.

Now, with the introduction of suspended sediments from continental runoff as well as increased nutrient loads from fertilizers and other chemical substances, the water takes on a milky cast. The turbidity increases with every mile, and as it does, the depth to which the sunlight is able to penetrate decreases steadily. Ten miles from the coast the surface is the color of robins' eggs. At the pilot area east of Cape Henelopen it is moss green, mixing in long, lazy tidal swirls with the gray-greens of the lower bay. At Miah Maull Shoal, twenty-five miles into the estuary, it is olive drab, with crests that look like whipped cream, and thirty miles farther west, at the site of the New Jersey Public Service Electric and Gas Company's 3,400-megawatt nuclear generating station (and the locus of maximum turbidity in the estuary), it is the color of café au lait.

There are many reasons for these changes in the color of the water, some as old as the sea itself, some much more recent and directly attributable to human activity and the press of human population. Ever since the Alleghenian orogeny three hundred million years ago, the Delaware estuary, like all large continental drainage basins, has carried millions of tons of suspended sediments annually from the coastal foothills down to the sea. There has always been an area of high turbidity about sixty miles into the estuary, for it is here that the cooler, saltier layers of seawater are forced to sink to the bottom while the fresher, sediment-laden layers of river water ride overtop.

Several hundred years ago, before the arrival of the first Westerners, a number of natural processes helped to control the runoff of sediments and to keep the river system clean. Dense hardwood forests covered the land upriver, and their root systems held the soils in check.

Thousands of square miles of salt marsh washed the seawater all along the fringes of the bay downstream. Oyster beds covered nearly every shoal from the bay mouth to the top of the tide, and billions of oysters siphoning trillions of gallons of water served as a natural filtering system.

Suspended sediments, when they did enter the estuary, carried no industrial toxins, no DDT or other pesticides, no elevated levels of arsenic, chromium, copper, lead, mercury, or other heavy metals, no polychlorinated biphenyls (PCB's), no nitrogen or phosphorus-loading from urban wastewater and agricultural runoff. Fish populations were healthy. Benthic communities, including the oyster beds, received adequate sunlight and nutrient levels and appropriate amounts of dissolved oxygen in order to maintain a rich diversification of species.

All this was about to change, however. A period of rapid urban growth and industrialization along the shores of the Delaware River and the upper watershed during the nineteenth and early twentieth centuries resulted, by 1950, in one of the most polluted stretches of river in the world. Water quality had been severely degraded. Habitat had been destroyed. Fish tissues had become toxic. The oyster beds were being threatened by a series of mysterious diseases. Human beings were being told that they could neither fish nor swim in large sections of the river and upper bay. The estuary was in crisis, and a serious cleanup effort was initiated.

The Delaware that John and I sail today is much improved over its degraded state of a few decades ago, although as the gateway to the world's largest freshwater port and the second-largest petrochemical refining center in the United States, it continues to be plagued by problems. The oyster beds are gone now throughout the lower bay, victims of the dermo and MSX parasites. Fish tissue advisories and no-consumption advisories continue to be issued by all three state fisheries agencies of Delaware, New Jersey, and Pennsylvania. Bottom grasses and other benthic flora continue to be threatened by high turbidity levels, toxins in the bottom sediments, and other chemical factors that inhibit photosynthesis. The combined effects of the twenty million human beings who live and work in the watershed still impact every dimension of the estuarian system.

Five miles past the nuclear generating station is the entrance to the C and D Canal, a fifteen-mile land cut that joins the Delaware River to the headwaters of the Chesapeake Bay. It is just after three o'clock in the afternoon as *Brendan* swings out of the tidal stream in the center of the river and crosses into an area of turbulence between a pair of rock jetties. Here, within a space of a few hundred yards, the coffee-colored water of the Delaware mixes with an even darker body of water that has flooded through the canal from the upper Chesapeake and that is the color of chocolate pudding.

Brendan proceeds under power now, pushing a curling wave of dark brown water ahead of her. John and I exchange places at the helm every couple of hours to steer around increasing numbers of small pleasure craft, a trio of tugs and barges, and a large automotive transport ship heading north out of the Port of Baltimore. After we leave the canal at its western end, we run along the perimeter of a dredged ship channel, then pass the mouth of the Susquehanna River at Turkey Point. Here we enter another area of high turbidity, this one defined by the confluence of salty bottom layers from the lower Chesapeake and fresh, muddy surface layers flowing out of the Susquehanna River system.

Many of the same factors that affect water quality in the Delaware estuary are reproduced here: deforestation, loss of shellfish beds, destruction of wetlands, rapid urban growth, intensive industrialization of upstream areas. Here in the Chesapeake, however, another set of factors also comes into play, for here, a hundred fifty miles from the sea, there is very little exchange of water by tidal action. This situation, when combined with high nutrient levels and very warm summer water temperatures, provides a perfect setting for eutrophic blooms of algae or other microorganisms that can choke off light and eradicate entire ecosystems. One such bloom—of a dangerous and poorly understood dinoflagellate called *pfiesteria*—has been making newspaper headlines all summer. This is the organism that has been blamed for massive fish kills—and perhaps also for injuries to the human central nervous system—in several of the rivers to our south.

As *Brendan* doubles the last headland and enters an area of shallows at the mouth of the Sassafras River, the water color changes one final time. The browns we had been staring at in the C and D Canal only a few miles back have disappeared, and in their place appears an undulating ribbon of jade green. At first the water seems clear, as if a miracle has taken place and we have retreated to the shelf break, two hundred miles back. Then I realize that the late afternoon sun is playing tricks with our eyes. The river water here *appears* green—but it is in fact opaque, with no penetration of the light beyond the dense concentrations of algae growing at its surface.

I say nothing to John. Like all the other water colors we have been witness to during the past thirty hours, this is one that we have seen before. I try to convince myself that it is harmless and presents no cause for concern— that it is a local anomaly, a function of the hot, dry Chesapeake summer. I peer ahead, straining for a glimpse of a familiar building or the figure of a loved one standing on the pier in front of our farm—and I know that I am wrong. As so many others, this color is a signal—a wake-up call—a part of the bittersweet experience of sailing home.

Poems in the Lap of Death

I was reading recently in an old anthology of American poetry when I happened across a disturbing little poem by E. E. Cummings—the poet, you may recall, whose trademark was that he almost never used capital letters or punctuation marks in his writing. I repeat several stanzas of the poem here—partly because they are clever and provocative, partly because they comprise one of the most thoroughly misanthropic utterances I've read in a long time.

Humanity i love you
because you would rather black the boots of
success than enquire whose soul dangles from his
watch-chain . . .

Humanity i love you because
when you're hard up you pawn your
intelligence to buy a drink . . .

Humanity i love you because you
are perpetually putting the secret of
life in your pants and forgetting
it's there and sitting down

on it
and because you are
forever making poems in the lap
of death Humanity

i hate you

    Misanthropic: a word derived from two Greek roots, *misein*, to hate, and *anthropos*, humankind. A misanthrope is, therefore, a hater of humankind, a despiser of his own DNA. There are plenty of misanthropes around these days, and for many good reasons—reasons that continue to multiply, along with our own numbers, exponentially.

Indeed, how is it possible to confront the growing body of evidence about what humanity is doing to itself and to the Earth and not become a misanthrope? How is it possible to look at a clear-cut mountainside or count the dead seabirds washed ashore after an oil spill or gaze upon a photograph of starving children or inhale the acrid stench of industrial smokestacks or watch an estuary suffocate on mats of floating algae—and not wish to turn your back on your own species?

Ten thousand years ago, at the end of the last ice age, an odd thing happened to a small population of hairless bipedal creatures who had survived the glaciers of the past one hundred thousand years as cave dwellers and wandering bands of hunter-gatherers. As the ice receded for the last time, these large-brained bipeds learned to plant and cultivate grain. In so doing, they created the conditions necessary for a profound self-transformation, from cave dwellers to villagers, from wanderers to permanent residents, from creatures of nature to creatures of culture.

History was born in that self-transforming moment, as were the transcendental religions and the personal God. Humankind became self-consciously separate from nature in that moment, eventually coming to understand itself as a fabricator, a manipulator, a user of the Earth. As we grew more technologically proficient, we became the self-proclaimed proprietors of all that we surveyed.

We told ourselves that we were the chosen species, created in God's image, destined to control and dominate and to take from the Earth whatever and wherever and whenever we wished.

For nearly ten thousand years nature appeared boundless and the actions of humankind seemed comparatively insignificant. And then our excesses began to catch up with us, even as we also continued to multiply at an ever-increasing rate. Our appetites led to the extinction of entire species. Our factories poisoned lakes and forests. Our technologies transformed the atmosphere and began to affect the very climate system upon which our continued survival on Earth depended.

The purgatory of our present generation, as one of my most misanthropic friends has observed, is the thought that we may soon become witnesses to our own extinction. (Perhaps an even more despairing thought is that we may *not* become witnesses to our own extinction but will leave that moment, as our most telling bequest, to our children.)

And what does all this mean?—that we as human beings are morally reprehensible? That we are environmental rapists and species murderers? That we are greedy, stupid, impulsive, uncaring, selfish creatures who would best be buried in a layer of plastic containers and aluminum pop-tops and forgotten in the ongoing process of natural selection?

Some would argue so—and they would seem to have a rather large body of evidence to support their case. But in spite of the evidence, I would side with those who take a more conciliatory view. In the midst of the squalor we have collectively visited on this planet, we are more than just a motley collection of vandals and thieves. We are also billions of individual people, doing the best we can, full of heroism, sacrifice, and love.

Jacques Cousteau once described humankind as the species who has dared to defy the fundamental laws of nature. For ten thousand years, ever since the agricultural revolution, we have been the rebels of the Earth. The odds have always been stacked against us, but in spite of this fact, our rebellion has been heroic—only our hubris has been ugly and small.

Pity us, poor human beings, for we are up against the wall. We are between a rock and a hard place. In front of us is the specter of our own self-annihilation as we foul the planet that has sustained us. But behind us, pushing against us, are ten thousand years of what we call our "civilization": our history, our religious mythos, our science, our political philosophy, our vision of millennial sociogenesis.

The challenge, for this most prideful and self-assured of rebels, is to effect the most profound rebellion of all— a rebellion against the very notion of ourselves as rebels, against our insistence that we are separate and unique and somehow superior to all the rest of nature.

Here is the ultimate challenge for the species who has assumed for five hundred generations that it has already met the ultimate challenge. Can we learn biological humility? Can we redirect the rebel within us and learn to abhor our own self-flattering histories and theologies and to think of ourselves (as Father Thomas Berry says) "as a species"? Can we cope with this kind of mythic demotion: from masters of the universe down to some kind of lowly apprentices again?

The answer is: it's still too soon to say. One suspects that many of us will not be able or willing to effect this final rebellion, this ultimate retransformation of ourselves back into one species among many. But might some of us? Is there still enough of this kind of heroism and sacrifice and love left in humanity? And if some of us can, will these become leaders with enough strength and courage and force of will to cause others to follow?

The story isn't over yet. There are still agendas to be written, choices to be made, actions to be carried out. This is why there is not yet room for despair. And this is why I'll not yet become a misanthrope, a despiser of my own DNA.

But I will make "poems in the lap of death"—why not? Poems, after all, are part of the spiritual apparatus we employ to define ourselves—and—why not?—to *re-*

define ourselves. (And anyhow, it's fun to imitate E. E.
Cummings and write without punctuation marks or capital letters.)

> Humanity i hate you
> because you are forever challenging
> the natural order within which you
> must exist . . .

> Humanity i hate you because
> you learn so quickly to adapt, until you learn
> to adapt to the conditions of your own
> extinction . . .

> Humanity i hate you because you
> will not set aside for the
> future—even when it is for the future of
> your own children . . .

> and because you also know these things
> and because you weep in the privacy of your fears
> and because you dream of Eden and conjure
> perfect worlds humanity

> i love you

Bibliography and Further Reading

Some readers of these essays may be curious about the sources of epigraphs and other references scattered throughout the text. Below is a bibliography of the most important of these sources, as well as a brief selection of further titles that may also be useful to readers who wish to pursue some of the ideas they have encountered in these pages.

ABBEY, EDWARD. *Desert Solitaire*, New York: McGraw Hill, 1968.

———. *Down the River*, New York: E. P. Dutton, 1982.

BERRY, THOMAS. *The Dream of the Earth*, San Francisco: Sierra Club Books, 1988.

CHATWIN, BRUCE. *The Songlines*, New York: Elisabeth Sifton Books/Viking, 1987.

Comprehensive Conservation Management Plan for the Delaware Estuary, Delaware Estuary Program, September 1996.

Bibliography

CUMMINGS, E. E. *Complete Poems 1904–1962,* ed. George J. Firmage, New York: Liveright Publishing Corp., 1991.

DENNETT, DANIEL C. *Darwin's Dangerous Idea: Evolution and the Meaning of life,* New York: Simon & Schuster, 1995.

DEVALL, BILL, and GEORGE SESSIONS. *Deep Ecology: Living as if Nature Mattered,* Salt Lake City: Peregrine Smith Books, 1985.

DILLARD, ANNIE. *Pilgrim at Tinker Creek,* New York: Harper and Row, 1974.

GLEICK, JAMES. *Chaos: The Making of a New Science,* New York: Viking, 1987.

GORDON, ANITA, and DAVID SUZUKI. *It's a Matter of Survival,* Cambridge, Mass.: Harvard University Press, 1991.

LOVELOCK, JAMES. *The Ages of Gaia: A Biography of Our Living Earth,* New York: Norton, 1988.

MOWAT, FARLEY. *Sea of Slaughter,* Boston: Atlantic Monthly Press, 1984.

QUINN, DANIEL. *Ishmael,* New York: Bantam, 1992.

ROSZAK, THEODORE. *Where the Wasteland Ends: Politics and Transcendence in Postindustrial Society,* New York: Doubleday, 1972.

THOMAS, LEWIS. *The Lives of a Cell: Notes of a Biology Watcher,* New York: Viking, 1974.

———. *The Fragile Species,* New York: Macmillan, 1992.

THOREAU, HENRY DAVID. *Walking,* New York: HarperCollins (paperback reprint), 1994.

Bibliography

WATTS, ALAN. *The Wisom of Insecurity: A Message for an Age of Anxiety*, New York: Pantheon, 1951.

World Population Data Sheet, Washington, D.C.: Population Reference Bureau, published annually.

"A gripping sea yarn tinged with disquieting scenarios
of cataclysmic climate change."
—*Outside*

RIDDLE OF THE ICE
A Scientific Adventure into the Arctic

This nautical adventure set aboard a fifty-foot sailboat
charts the bleakest and most awesome landscape on earth—
and one man's fierce will to understand it. By any account,
the impenetrable barrier of sea ice that blocked the passage
of the *Brendan's Isle* should not have been there in July,
especially in the midst of one of the hottest summers on
record. Frustrated and mystified at having to turn back so
early in his northbound voyage, sailor Myron Arms became
determined to explain the unsettling anomaly.

Three years later, having pursued this obsession from
the Woods Hole Oceanographic Institution to NASA's
Goddard Space Flight Center, Arms took his boat and small
crew back up the Labrador Coast to test his ideas—this time
making it past the Arctic Circle.

Travel/Environmental Science/Sailing/0-385-49093-3

ANCHOR BOOKS

Visit Anchor on the web at www.anchorbooks.com
Available at your local bookstore, or call toll-free to order:
1-800-793-2665 (credit cards only).

Printed in the United States
by Baker & Taylor Publisher Services